500
WORDS
YOU SHOULD
KNOW

CAROLINE TAGGART

Michael O'Mara Books Limited

First published in Great Britain in 2014 by
Michael O'Mara Books Limited
9 Lion Yard
Tremadoc Road
London SW4 7NQ

A CIP catalogue record for this book is available from the British
Library.

Papers used by Michael O'Mara Books Limited are natural,
recyclable products made from wood grown in sustainable
forests. The manufacturing processes conform to the
environmental regulations of the country of origin.

ISBN: 978-1-78243-294-4 in hardback print format
ISBN: 978-1-78243-298-2 in e-book format

1 2 3 4 5 6 7 8 9 10

Typeset by K.DESIGN, Winscombe, Somerset
Printed and bound by CPI Group (UK) Ltd, Croydon, CR0 4YY

www.mombooks.com

Contents

Introduction

This is a book for the logophile – the lover of words. When selecting words to include, I deliberately avoided the technical, the highly specialized and the overly obscure. You will seek in vain in these pages for *adiabatic, haptotropism* or *phosphorylation*; nor will you find *byssus, facinorous* or *thigmophilic*. My attitude to the former group is that if you need to know them you probably know them already and to the latter that you are not easily going to work them into your day-to-day conversation.

Come to think of it, you won't find *logophile* here either.

No, what I have tried to do is pick things that made me think, 'Ooh, that's a nice word' (an approach, I may tell you, that played havoc with my reading and my conversation for a number of weeks). Most of my 500 choices will be familiar, at least vaguely, to most of you. They may include words you have forgotten you knew, or words you are uncomfortable about using because you aren't 100 per cent sure of their meaning. Our media don't always help us in this regard. Words, of course, do change their meaning with the passage of time and some of those I have written about seem to have been given a new lease of life lately, not necessarily through being used 'correctly'. HUBRIS and

KUDOS come to mind, and, as I have said in the text, I expect to receive angry letters for my views on DECIMATE.

If this book has any instructive purpose, it's to help you to work out the meanings of unfamiliar words through their similarity to familiar ones. If you know, for example, that *anthropology* is the study of humankind, you can begin to have a guess at what a MISANTHROPIST is and what ANTHROPOMORPHIC means, just by taking note of the recurring elements in each word. I've also tried to clarify some areas of confusion by pointing out, for example, that NOISOME is nothing to do with noise nor ESCHEW with chewing.

But really this is not a book that is intended to teach or to preach. Yes, it aims to help you use words correctly and to enrich what I am sure is already a rich vocabulary. Most of all, however, it hopes to stop you briefly in your tracks as you flick through its pages and say, as I have done, 'Ooh, that's a nice word.'

Between us, we can keep logophilia alive and well.

Caroline Taggart
May 2014

CHAPTER ONE

Terms of Endearment, Respect and Admiration

The compliments and accolades included here range from admiration of intellect to appreciation of sexual attraction, but it's intriguing that this should be the shortest chapter in the book. Are we really so unimaginative when it comes to being nice to people? Even this brief list includes attributes that become boring or annoying if taken too far.

adroit

History – or word usage at least – has a long-standing prejudice against left-handedness: *gauche* (the French word for left) is used in English to mean physically clumsy or socially inept, whereas *sinister* (the Latin) is – well, sinister. There is even the word *gaucherie,* meaning an awkward or tactless remark. On the other side of the coin, as it were, we have *dextrous* (from the Latin for right), meaning the very opposite of clumsy, likely to take a catch that the gauche person would have dropped, and *adroit* (from the French), adept, tactful, immune from the awkwardness and tendency to gaffes that characterize the gauche person. To make matters worse, a tactless or unsubtle person may also be described as *maladroit*: 'badly right'.

aspiration

To aspire to something is to long to achieve it, particularly if it may be beyond your reach: 'He *aspires* to be CEO of a company, but he has neither the brains nor the charisma.' Such a desire is an *aspiration*: 'To become a CEO has always been his greatest *aspiration*.'

assiduous

You can take *assiduity* too far – someone who didn't return your affection wouldn't thank you for being *assiduous in your attentions* – but on the whole it is a good thing, meaning hard-working and persevering. *An assiduous researcher* is one who isn't put off by a lack of early success, while *an assiduous reader* spends every available moment with a book. Reading is a particularly appropriate thing to do assiduously, as the word comes from the Latin for 'to sit down to', with the sense of putting your nose to the grindstone.

∽≋∾

avuncular

Literally 'pertaining to an uncle': affectionate and helpful to someone younger. The word is usually applied not to the young person's relatives but to a family friend or perhaps an older boss. There is no suggestion of impropriety here: *He had an avuncular attitude to the children's antics* simply means he enjoyed watching them and didn't object to their jumping on the furniture; when they were a bit older he might take *an avuncular interest in their careers*, recommending them to friends who might employ bright young things.

As for a female equivalent, the OED gives *materteral*, but describes it as humorous and rare; it's clearly been made up by someone who has a MODICUM of Latin and thinks there darn well *ought* to be a word. In the modern, non-Latin-speaking world, you're probably safer sticking to the unexciting *auntly* if you want people to know what you mean.

∽≋∾

benevolent

Not a million miles from *benign* (see under MALIGNANT), this literally means 'well-wishing' but has a sense of being more active than that – not only well-wishing but doing something about it. *A benevolent dictator* doesn't just sit around smiling. Nor, come to that, does the opposite: *a malevolent dictator* is much more likely to instigate an invasion or conduct a purge than he is to stay in the office scowling.

burgeoning

To burgeon is to grow healthily and rapidly, to flourish. Originally used of plants, it can now refer to anything from *Brazil's burgeoning economy* to *a burgeoning romance* or *a burgeoning interest in social reform*.

callipygian

You might not often need a word for 'having a nice backside', but when you do, this is it. In fact it's one of two: you might prefer *callipygous*. The stress in both words is on the *pyg*; in *callipygian* the *g* is pronounced as a *j*; in *callipygous* it is a hard sound as in *girl*. Specifically, they mean having well-developed, round buttocks. *Calli-* comes from the Greek for beautiful (as in *calligraphy*, beautiful writing) and the rest of the word relates to the buttocks. It doesn't occur in any common English words, although ornithologists may like to know that *pygopod birds* such as diving ducks have their legs placed a long way back on the body, near what would be their buttocks if they had such things.

cognoscenti

'Those in the know', from the Italian for *knowing*, usually about the arts: a sixteen-hour performance of Wagner's *Ring Cycle* might be expected to appeal to the *cognoscenti* – those who appreciate the finer points of the work. The word may also be used in a less high-brow context: 'Parking at the racecourse is a nightmare, so the *cognoscenti* park at the supermarket and walk the last 200 yards.'

complement

This spelling of the word means to make complete and it has various technical meanings in maths and grammar; in non-tech speech it means little more than to go together well: 'That blue dress really *complements* your eyes.' That remark is, of course, a *compliment*, which 'That red dress really *complements* your eyes' probably isn't.

☙❧

coruscating

This means flashy or sparkling and may be used to describe a flashy or sparkling personality or argument. The Victorian essayist Thomas Carlyle wrote of John Sterling, a writer friend who had died young, 'Like a swift dashing meteor he came into our circle; *coruscated* among us, for a day or two.' The adjective is also often applied to the wit of Oscar Wilde, perhaps not entirely flatteringly.

☙❧

doyen

This is the masculine form; the feminine is *doyenne*. They are French words for the leader of a group, perhaps of academics; the senior or most distinguished member of a certain body. Thus you might speak of *the doyen of the English department*, *the doyenne of theatrical agents* or *the doyen of travel documentaries.* It's a respectful term, but don't be surprised if you hear next year that the person has retired. See also EMERITUS, opposite.

☙❧

dulcet

Pronounced *dull-set*, but a much prettier word than that suggests: it means sweet-sounding. It's often used ironically: 'I thought I recognized your *dulcet* tones' needn't mean much more than, 'Oh, there you are.' But it may also be employed sincerely to describe things of great beauty: Oberon in *A Midsummer Night's Dream* recalls hearing:

> a mermaid on a dolphin's back
> Uttering such *dulcet* and harmonious breath,
> That the rude sea grew civil at her song.

Of course, seeing mermaids on dolphins' backs doesn't happen often nowadays (unless, perhaps, you are king of the fairies), which may be why the irony has set in.

⚬≈⚬

emeritus

From the Latin meaning 'thoroughly deserved', this is normally a title given to a semi-retired academic. *A professor emeritus* is expected neither to teach a full complement of classes nor to continue with administrative duties, but is still called a professor because of long and honourable service. You might, if you were being disrespectful, say it was the scholarly equivalent of being kicked upstairs.

⚬≈⚬

emulate

To imitate in a competitive way, to aim to outstrip or out-achieve: 'However good a tennis player I become, I am never going to *emulate* Roger Federer' or 'I would love to *emulate* her style, but I would look ridiculous in a dress as close-fitting as that.' Something done *in a spirit of emulation* is done in an attempt to beat someone else, but with an element of respect mingled with the competitiveness.

⚬≈⚬

encomium

From the Greek for festivity, this is a formal expression of praise, not unlike a PANEGYRIC (see page 19): you might *utter an encomium* on the retirement of someone distinguished or *heap encomiums* on a particularly good play. The word can be a bit high-flown, but Dickens, as so often, brought it down to earth: in *The Old Curiosity Shop* he has a hospitable character bring in bread, cheese and beer, 'with many high *encomiums* upon their excellence'.

erudite

From the Latin for polished, this means scholarly, learned, well-read. 'We had a particularly *erudite* Latin teacher who knew Cicero by heart and could also quote reams of Homer in Greek'; or 'His explanation of the use of the present perfect continuous tense sounded very *erudite*, but it was way above my head.'

euphemism

A nice or inoffensive way of saying something potentially unpleasant or embarrassing, such as 'passed away' for 'died' or 'smallest room' for 'toilet'. The prefix *eu-* (pronounced 'you') means pleasant, and recurs in words such as *euphony*, a pleasing sound in speech; *euphoria*, literally 'a good ability to endure', hence an exaggerated feeling of joy; and, appallingly, *eugenics*, from the Greek for 'well born' and meaning a way of 'improving' the quality of the human race by stopping the people you don't approve of from reproducing.

The opposite of a euphemism is a *dysphemism*, deliberately saying something in an unpleasant or unsympathetic way: 'kicked the bucket' or 'snuffed it' are *dysphemisms* for 'died'. See also DYSTOPIA.

꩜

felicitous

Deriving from the Latin for 'happy', this normally applies to a remark and means 'appropriate, expressed in well-chosen words'. It's often used in a negative sense: if someone tells you that what you have just said was *not entirely felicitous,* you can be reasonably confident that you have put your foot in it. Sending someone *felicitations* – wishing them happiness – on their engagement comes from the same source, as does the rather old-fashioned word *felicity* ('When shall we have the *felicity* of seeing you here again?').

꩜

gregarious

Grex is the Latin for a flock and a *gregarious* animal is one, like a sheep or cow, that lives in a flock or herd. By extension, *a gregarious person* is never happier than when surrounded by others, going to parties, meeting new people. Karl Marx thought that this was part of the human condition – 'The human being is in the most literal sense a political animal, not merely a gregarious animal, but an animal which can individuate itself only in the midst of society' – and who am I to argue?

From the same root comes *egregious*, standing out from the crowd, often in a bad way: 'He's an *egregious* example of the jealous husband – he doesn't trust her to go anywhere without him' or 'If you rely on the spellchecker rather than proofreading your work yourself you will let some *egregious* errors slip through.'

impeccable

Literally 'unable to sin', this more usually means 'faultless' and can apply to anything from your dress sense and DEMEANOUR (*impeccably turned out, impeccable manners*) to your career path (*an impeccable track record*), your taste (*an impeccable choice of music/restaurant/soft furnishings*) and your thinking on key issues (*impeccable logic*). The author Mordecai Richler put it neatly when he said, 'Coming from Canada, being a writer and Jewish as well, I have *impeccable* paranoia credentials.'

❦

indispensable

That which cannot be dispensed with, can't be done without. A particularly good guidebook might be described as *indispensable for* (or *to*) *the visitor to Rome*; while a good pair of binoculars might be *indispensable to the birdwatcher* and the United Nations might play *an indispensable role in the peace negotiations*.

❦

inimitable

That cannot be imitated, in a class of its own – used very much in an admiring way. A collection of P. G. Wodehouse's short stories about the 'gentleman's gentleman' *par excellence* is called *The Inimitable Jeeves*; it's an adjective that has also been applied to a range of Chanel eye make-up, to many actors, artists and writers (*the inimitable John Steinbeck*), and to dressmaking, which the designer Christian Dior described as '... in a machine age ... one of the last refuges of the human, the personal, the inimitable'.

Inimitable is not to be confused with *inimical*, which means adverse, unfriendly, hostile. This is a forceful word:

inimical feelings are not just mildly, indifferently unfriendly, they are positively, actively antagonistic. *Inimicable* does exist and means the same as *inimical*, but is rare, so if you do come across it, it may well be being used by mistake.

❦

kudos

This is a word that seems suddenly to have come out of its box and be dancing around everywhere, used in expressions such as 'Kudos to X' to mean 'Congratulations to X', 'Full marks to X', as if it were an exclamation. More accurately, *kudos* means acclaim or prestige: it's something you earn through hard work, generosity or some other such praiseworthy quality. The actor Kenneth Branagh is quoted as saying that being associated with Shakespeare gives you *some kind of bogus kudos,* whereas the hairdresser Vidal Sassoon complained that his profession wasn't recognized as a worthy craft or *given the kudos it deserved.*

❦

magnanimous

A word beginning *magn-* (unless it's related to *magnets* or *magnesium*, which mean something completely different) is likely to convey size or greatness in one sense or another. To *magnify* is to make bigger, *magnificence* is grandeur and *magnitude* is to do with relative size. The *-animus* part of *magnanimous* refers to the soul, so *a magnanimous person* is big-hearted, generous, and *a magnanimous gesture* is one that forgives and forgets (either a financial debt or an affront).

❦

mellifluous

Literally 'flowing with honey', this is often used to describe the rich tones of an actor known for the beauty of his voice. Oddly, the actor is usually a he: think James Mason or, more recently, Morgan Freeman.

❧

meticulous

While being either FASTIDIOUS or ASSIDUOUS can be overdone and therefore borderline good/bad, *meticulousness* is praiseworthy unless you are really in a rush. *A meticulous person* cannot be hurried: he or she wants to check every detail, make sure all the arrangements are in place. The word can also be applied to the person's actions, as in *a meticulous search of the premises*, leaving no paperclip unturned, or a *meticulous arrangement of flowers,* in which each one is in perfect symmetry.

❧

momentous

Very important, of great moment. The cliché use is *on this momentous occasion,* often as part of a wedding speech or award ceremony. *Momentous* is not to be confused with *momentary*, which means lasting only a moment: *a momentary lapse of concentration*. There is a considerable transatlantic divide in the use of the adverb *momentarily*: British English says this too means *lasting* only a moment: 'The bird landed *momentarily* on the gatepost but flew off again in a flash'; in America it means *in* just a moment: 'I'm nearly ready; I'll do it *momentarily*.' This latter usage is drifting inexorably across the Atlantic, but still makes many Brits squirm.

❧

paean

A *paean* (pronounced *pee-an*) was in Ancient Greece a song sung in praise or thanks to a god; nowadays it is any form of extravagant praise, as in 'The whole review was a *paean* to the author's past achievements and didn't tell me a thing about the new book.'

palatable

The *palate* – the roof of the mouth – is associated with the sense of taste, so to have *a palate for fine food* is to be something of a *gourmet* (see GOURMAND). Food or drink that is *palatable*, therefore, is easy on the palate, pleasant to the taste buds (most of our 10,000 taste buds are in fact found on the tongue, but there are some on the palate and we are in the realms of metaphor here, so let's not be picky). Be careful how you use this word: to describe a wine as *palatable* to the host who has just poured it for you is a touch condescending. It's not only food and drink that can be palatable – you can put forward *palatable arguments* (ones that are likely to be acceptable to the other person) while a radio station that features popular arias is more *palatable* than one that insists on playing the whole opera.

panegyric

A public speech or piece of writing in praise of a person or thing; it derives from the Greek for *all* and *assembly* (see also *panacea* in the entry for ALCHEMY). In Elizabethan times, a writer might compose *a panegyric* to his patron when dedicating a book to him. Three centuries later Oscar Wilde, maintaining that it was not a publisher's role to boast about the quality of the books he published, objected to the idea of a work being accompanied by 'a premature and unnecessary *panegyric* from the publisher'.

෧෴෧

pellucid

Related to *lucid*, 'clear', with a prefix meaning through, this means 'shining through, very clear indeed'. A lake may be described as *pellucid,* if the water is so clean and still that you can see right to the bottom; so too may a writing style or an argument in which you understand every word.

෧෴෧

punctilious

This isn't a million miles from METICULOUS (see page 18), but tends to apply more to a careful observer of etiquette: a man in a costume drama might kiss a lady's hand *punctiliously*, not because he wanted to but because it was the correct thing to do. The rarely used word *punctilio* refers specifically to small points of etiquette – and indeed comes from the Italian for 'a small point'. *Punctual,* which originally meant being precise in every point (*the punctual performance of his duties)* before it narrowed down to 'turning up precisely on time'; *puncture* (caused by a small point or prick); and *punctuation* (making little marks on a page) all come from a similar pointy source.

෧෴෧

pundit

From the Hindi for a learned man, this word has been much debased and is now most often used of retired sports stars who earn a living analysing televised matches. There are also political pundits, stock-market pundits, racing pundits and pundits on almost any other subject where so-called expertise can fill television time or newspaper column inches. I've classed it as a term of respect, because that is how it started, but in today's PARLANCE it is borderline for a term of mild contempt.

෧෴෨

redoubtable

The redoubtable Mrs Thatcher, people said during her premiership; today they might apply the same adjective to Mrs Clinton or Mrs Merkel. It means formidable, deserving of a great deal of respect and taking no nonsense from anyone. A redoubtable person is often a woman, but doesn't have to be: you could have *a redoubtable opponent* (of either sex) in a tennis tournament or *a redoubtable agent* (likewise) negotiating a contract on your behalf. In the tennis match you'd have to be at your best; with the agent you could relax, confident that you would be getting a good deal.

෧෴෨

Rubensesque

The Flemish artist Sir Peter Paul Rubens (1577–1640) was renowned for – among many other talents – painting scantily dressed women who were a good 15 kilos heavier than they might have been had he been painting famous beauties today. The adjective derived from his name, therefore, is used to describe a full, well-rounded female form, or specific parts of it: *a Rubensesque bosom* or *Rubensesque hips*. The OED also gives the spelling *Rubenesque*, without saying it is wrong; it is certainly easier to pronounce, but the man's name was Rubens with an *s*, so it is really to that the *–esque* suffix should be added.

sapient

Wise, knowing, referring to some sort of innate understanding rather than acquired learning: *a sapient remark* reveals an insight into human nature that makes it quite different from an ERUDITE one. Modern use tends to be either self-consciously literary or ironic: 'He looked at me with a *sapient* eye' suggests that he knew I was going to get myself into trouble.

sonorous

At its most basic, this means making or capable of making a sound, but it is normally used to *describe* that sound – deep and imposing, like the ring of a heavy bell or the rich, many-layered voices of actors such as James Earl Jones and Christopher Lee.

urbane

There was a time when living in a city (Latin *urbs*, hence *urban*) meant you were highly cultured, while living in the country (Latin *rus*, hence *rural* and *rustic*) suggested you were unsophisticated, probably rough and ready in your manners and possibly stupid as well. This prejudice lives on in *urbane*, which means charming, courteous, suave, elegant of manner. It is almost always applied to a man: think George Clooney. See also BOORISH and CHURLISH.

versatile

Able to turn your hand to anything, adaptable. The British comedians Peter Cook and Dudley Moore once admiringly described chameleons as *versatile creatures*: they could 'take on the shape and colour of anything they like' so effectively that an acquaintance of Pete and Dud's had nearly married one. Sportspeople and other performers can also be versatile – a soccer player may be equally happy as a defender or in the midfield; an actor at home in both comedy and tragedy. The Swiss army knife is *a versatile tool*, as is a food processor with a number of attachments. In fact, this is a versatile word.

---

virtuoso

The Italian for learned or skilful, this usually describes a musician who is not only talented but has superb technique: 'Paganini was one of the greatest *virtuoso* violinists of all time.' It might also apply to a demanding piece of music, as in *a virtuoso clarinet solo,* which would allow the clarinettist to display his *virtuosity. Virtuoso* may also be a noun ('Paganini was a great *virtuoso*'), with the plural *virtuosi.*

---

vivacious

As URBANE is more often applied to a man, so *vivaciousness* or *vivacity* tends to be a characteristic of young women. *Vivacious* means lively, high spirited, and can be used to describe a person, their personality or other attributes, such as *a vivacious smile* or *a vivacious wave of the hand.* In small doses it's an endearing characteristic, but if you come across someone who is relentlessly vivacious you may find that a little of her company goes quite a long way.

CHAPTER TWO

Terms of Abuse, Criticism and Mild Contempt

This is an area in which the English language really lets its hair down, spits on its hands and gets stuck in. Whether we're accusing someone of bossiness, dishonesty, sexual depravity or just having bad taste, we let our imaginations run riot and our pens flow with vitriol.

amoral

This is often wrongly used as a synonym for *immoral*, but the distinction is worth preserving. The *immoral* person ignores morals, goes against accepted rules; the *amoral* one doesn't consider the rules relevant or even recognize that they exist. Some aspects of science, for instance, might be considered *amoral*, because they seek to push back the frontiers of understanding without regard for the consequences; but only an *immoral* scientist would use his knowledge to detonate remote-controlled bombs in public places.

animadversion

A strong criticism, a carefully considered but disparaging remark: 'Her *animadversions* on the male sex in general suggested she was angry with one man in particular.' The verb is *to animadvert*: 'He was always *animadverting* on the ills of capitalist society.' Both come from Latin words meaning 'to turn the mind against'.

antediluvian

Dating from before the Flood (the one with Noah's ark in it) and therefore very old or old-fashioned: 'My mother's *antediluvian* attitudes meant I was never allowed any stylish clothes.'

asperity

Sharpness or harshness, especially in your manner of speaking: '"That is not a suitable topic of conversation for the dinner table," she said with some *asperity*.'

atavistic

Used of an action or a development that occurred in the times of our remote ancestors and hasn't been repeated in the intervening generations. It's much used by botanists and anthropologists, but can also be applied more casually – 'Climbing the nearest tree was an *atavistic* response to the threat of being chased by wolves' – or as an alternative to outdated: 'The *atavistic* nationalism that led to two world wars has no place in twenty-first-century politics.'

❧

authoritarian

Having authority, but enforcing it tyrannically, in a 'you will do what I say' fashion. Not to be confused with *authoritative*, which means having authority in a reliable way. An *authoritative* figure commands respect through strength of personality; an *authoritarian* one gets his way through bullying.

❧

bellwether

A *wether* is a ram, often the leader of a flock and distinguished by the fact that he wears a bell. The rest of the sheep tend to follow him blindly, as sheep do. The same applies to a non-ovine *bellwether*, which might mean the (human) leader of a group whose followers don't bother to think about what they are following, or an inanimate trend that lures people in its wake: 'The *bellwether* of fashion insists that skirt lengths change every season.' But this use is rarer than it once was: a bellwether is now more commonly an indication of a trend, as in 'The graduates' poor performance in the job market is a worrying *bellwether* of declining standards in the college.'

blatant

Glaringly and offensively conspicuous: *a blatant attempt to cheat at exams* or *a blatant forgery* has no claim to subtlety. Quiz fact: the word was first used by the Elizabethan poet Edmund Spenser; his epic poem *The Faerie Queene* contains a character called the Blatant Beast who personifies the evil caused in the world by envy and scandalmongering. Why Spenser chose that particular word and where it comes from, no one seems to be sure.

❧

bombastic

It's tempting to assume this means 'likely to explode at any moment', but in fact *bombast* is an old word for 'a material used for padding' and the adjective now describes pompous or extravagant speech or language: *the bombastic style of your letter* or *a bombastic approach to lecturing* could both do with being toned down.

❧

boorish

A *boor* is a clumsy, insensitive person, usually a man, and his manners are likely to be *boorish*. This can cover anything from not saying please or thank you, to elbowing his way to the buffet table and grabbing all the chocolate chip cookies before anyone else. *Boorish behaviour* need not take place in public – it could be as simple as changing the television station in the middle of a show someone else is watching – but it's highly undesirable wherever it happens.

❧

byzantine

Relating to Byzantium, the ancient city on the site of modern Istanbul; hence a highly stylized form of art and architecture; and hence again, in a figurative sense, complicated and inflexible in attitude. A *byzantine legal system* is badly in need of reform; *the byzantine plot of a thriller* needs to be much simplified if the average reader is to understand it.

calumny

Another word for a strong criticism (see ANIMADVERSION, page 25), but this one is likely to be untrue: 'When he says I cheated in my exams, it's a *calumny*; I worked hard to get those results.' A person given to making such remarks, or the remarks themselves, could be described as *calumnious* or, more rarely but sounding more spiteful, *calumniatory*; the verb is *to calumniate*. *Vicious calumny* is often heard but is really a TAUTOLOGY: a calumny is almost by definition vicious.

cantankerous

One of those lovely words that means just what it sounds as if it should mean: bad-tempered, complaining, likely to pick a quarrel at the slightest provocation. It's frequently applied to an elderly person who refuses to move with the times: *a cantankerous old man* (or *woman* – there's nothing gender-specific about being cantankerous). If you are of an artistic bent, however, there may be a cure for the bad temper that too often comes with age: Vincent van Gogh is quoted as saying, 'The more ugly, older, more *cantankerous*, more ill and poorer I become, the more I try to make amends by making my [shades] more vibrant, more balanced and beaming.'

〜

capricious

Caprice is a French word that probably ultimately derives from the Latin for a goat and is therefore related to the zodiac sign Capricorn; its nearest English equivalent is *whim* and to be *capricious* is to be whimsical, impulsive, subject to sudden changes of mind. It may sound fun but does imply that you are also FICKLE and unreliable.

〜

catamite

Not a frequently used word, it sprang to fame in the 1980s with the publication of Anthony Burgess's novel *Earthly Powers*. 'It was the afternoon of my eighty-first birthday, and I was in bed with my *catamite* when Ali announced that the archbishop had come to see me,' read the first sentence, giving pause to those who always thought that 'It is a truth universally acknowledged ...' or 'Mother died today. Or maybe yesterday; I don't know' were the most striking opening lines in fiction. Catamite means the 'kept' young lover of a homosexual man, and it in this section because 'keeping' anyone is surely a self-indulgent thing to do.

〜

cavalier

A simplistic approach to the English Civil Wars shows the Cavaliers – the royalists, as opposed to the dour Puritanical supporters of Cromwell – arrayed in lace, with feathers in their hats, up for a good time. The modern sense of *cavalier* (which comes from the French meaning for horseman) is more negative than that; it means offhand and haughty, taking no notice of responsibilities or the feelings of others. You could have *a cavalier attitude* to anything from carbon emissions to getting to work on time; they both boil down to 'What the heck, why should I bother?' See also INSOUCIANT.

෨෨෧

censorious

In Ancient Rome there was an official called a *censor*, one of whose duties was to keep an eye on public morals (quite a challenge in Ancient Rome, you might think). The same title is given to the person who decides who is allowed to see which films, and to the army officer who reads soldiers' letters home and stops them from telling their mothers their exact location. There is also a verb, so a *censor's* duty is *to censor*. From all of this comes the adjective *censorious*, meaning highly critical, quick to find fault: telling a teenage daughter, 'You're not going out dressed like that' could be described as *a censorious remark*.

Not to be confused with *censor* is *censure* (again both a noun and a verb), meaning an expression of strong disapproval, often in a formal context. The *censorious* parent might *censure* her offspring's clothes – meaning she expresses her opinion in no uncertain terms – but she would *censor* them only if she made the girl go upstairs and change into something more modest.

෨෨෧

charlatan

A French word, with the initial sound pronounced *sh*, this means someone who lays claim to skills he doesn't have, especially in medicine: 'Any *charlatan* can put up a plaque and pretend to be an expert in Balinese herbs.' A charlatan can also be a fraud in other contexts, but then the word has an old-fashioned ring to it – the sort of person who might describe a man (and it is usually a man) as a charlatan might equally well call him a cad or a bounder and would certainly mean that the offending party was no gentleman.

churlish

A *churl* was originally an uneducated farm worker (English has a long tradition of assuming that townspeople have better manners than country ones – see also URBANE), and is similar to a boor (see BOORISH, page 27). *Churlish* has come to mean surly, ill-mannered, but in a quieter, more sulky way than *boorish*. A churlish person would refuse an invitation briefly and ungraciously; a boorish one might well say, 'Good God, no, wouldn't be seen dead at Katie's wedding. Can't stand the girl.'

contentious

Something that may be *contended* over or become a bone of *contention* is described as *contentious*: disputed, controversial or, when it refers to a person, argumentative. *A contentious question* may be anything from whether or not hunting should be banned to where you put the stress in your pronunciation of the word *controversy*: the point is that it will provoke heated argument.

covetous

As given by the Old Testament Book of Exodus, three of the Ten Commandments enjoin us not to *covet* things belonging to our neighbour – it means to envy him for owning them and desire to own them ourselves. So if we disobey these commandments we become *covetous* ourselves and probably *cast covetous eyes* on someone's house, wife, male servant, female servant, ox or donkey. The Commandments make no specific mention of money, fast cars or 3D TVs, but it's certainly possible to covet those, too.

◦❧◦

cupidinous

The Greek god of love was Eros, and words derived from his name, such as *erotic, erotica* and *erogenous zones*, are connected with love and sex. Eros's Roman equivalent was Cupid and, despite the famously enamouring effects of Cupid's arrows, *cupidinous* desires are likely to be for money or possessions rather than for anything more intimate.

Dr Johnson's (eighteenth-century) dictionary defines *cupidity* as 'concupiscence; unlawful or unreasonable longing', but, as so often with Dr Johnson, that isn't immensely helpful, because *concupiscence* can mean all sorts of desire. A sixteenth-century translation of the Bible uses *concupiscence* where the Authorized Version, a hundred years later, has 'lust' instead and the twentieth-century New International Version has 'evil desire'; I think we know what is meant there. But in the seventeenth century, the poet and satirist Samuel Butler used the word in the broader sense: 'A Litigious Man goes to Law … to spend his Money, and satisfy his *Concupiscence* of Wrangling.' Either way, both cupidity and concupiscence are bad things and you should certainly try to keep more control of yourself.

૯≋૭

decrepit

Very old, worn down and creaky; used to describe a person, a building or possibly a philosophy or political policy that has outlived its usefulness. As the nineteenth-century poet Walter Savage Landor put it, 'States, like men, have their growth, their manhood, their *decrepitude*, their decay.' It's time they were put out to grass is the subtext.

૯≋૭

denounce

To accuse publicly, to give information against. A serious word: you are likely to *denounce someone as a traitor, a hypocrite* or, at best, *a fool.*

૯≋૭

deprecate

To express disapproval, to criticize. It isn't as public as to DENOUNCE (see previous entry): you could *deprecate someone's hypocrisy* (or *foolishness*) in private. *To depreciate* is similar, but carries the implication that your criticism has reduced someone's worth – it's related to the *depreciation* that attacks the value of your new car. *Self deprecation*, however, is to undervalue yourself, often jokingly.

૯≋૭

derisory

An adjective applied to a very small amount, often, but not necessarily of, money. It's connected with *derision* and is therefore such a small amount that it deserves to be laughed at. *Derisive* is another close relation and is usually applied to something mocking or scornful. *A derisive account* of the pay negotiations, for example, might explain why staff received *a derisory salary increase.*

❧

desultory

Half-hearted, unmethodical, without really paying attention. Not generally used to describe a person, this is found in expressions such as *in a desultory manner* or, memorably in a 1940s detective novel by Georgette Heyer, *the flirtation was a desultory affair*, because one of the participants was worrying about the murder rather than paying attention to the girl who was attempting to flirt with him.

❧

diatribe

A forceful, bitter criticism; a rant. Opposition parties have been known to indulge in *anti-government diatribes,* and diatribes may also be aimed at anything from religious beliefs you don't happen to share to fellow academics with whom you disagree on a minor point. Be warned: if you are indulging in a diatribe you are almost certainly getting carried away and may be close to losing your temper. It may be worth taking a moment to calm down.

❧

didactic

From the Greek for teaching, this means instructive, conveying a message (perhaps a political or moral one) or opinion. Although this concept was originally interpreted as being good for us, the modern meaning implies that the teaching is excessive, heavy-handed, not to be argued with: 'I hate his *didactic* way of talking about wine, as if he were the only person who knew one grape from another.'

⌇

disquisition

A *disquisition* may be spoken or written, but either way it is a long, formal and in-depth study of a subject. It's likely to be learned, authoritative, possibly moralizing and probably just a bit boring.

⌇

draconian

Draco was an Ancient Athenian politician who introduced a code of laws according to which a startling number of crimes were punishable by death. The adjective derived from his name therefore means exceedingly strict, severe. It's most often used to describe such things as discipline, punishment, rules and regulations, but if a person whose views on these things were harsh they could be accused of having *draconian attitudes*, or indeed of being *draconian* himself.

⌇

effrontery

Cheek, insolence, as in 'He had the *effrontery* to say I never give him anything after I paid for his whole family to go on holiday last year.' Not to be confused with *affronted*, meaning offended, which is how the person uttering that last complaint might feel.

⌇

enormity

A commonly misused word, this does not mean
enormousness. It means appallingness, great wickedness.
'He seemed not to realize the *enormity* of his crime' means
he didn't acknowledge he had done something dreadful,
but not necessarily that he had wiped out an entire city.

❦

ersatz

From the German for 'replacement', this is an adjective
describing an inferior imitation of something more
valuable or attractive: 'It was one of those twee little hotels
with *ersatz* Victorian furniture' or '*Ersatz* lemon meringue
pie, made with some awful artificial lemon substitute.'

❦

etiolated

In the plant world, this describes a green plant that has gone
pale through lack of sunlight; in human terms it means pale
and weak: 'His skin had that *etiolated* look of a video-game
player who has spent his youth on his game console.'

❦

excoriate

Even harsher than DENOUNCE, this means literally to take
the skin off, so metaphorically to flay someone alive, to
criticize very severely. A critic might, for example, write
an excoriating review of a film or play he loathed, while
an angry politician might make *an excoriating criticism* of
government policy.

❦

extravaganza

An Italian word, this time related to *extravagance* and meaning a very showy and elaborate performance, the sort of thing that might have been put on by Hollywood director Busby Berkeley or a flamboyant West End or Broadway producer. Special effects, fancy costumes, fireworks – you name it, an extravaganza has it. Expense is no object and taste is rarely a consideration.

◦◕◙◦

facile

An extract from the *Atlantic Monthly* dated 1900 gives a particularly damning use of this word: 'The English drawing master did not teach art, but *facile* tricks of the brush.' *Facile* comes from the Latin for easy and did once mean just that. In modern usage, however, it has the added sense of being just a bit too easy and thus having little value: *a facile victory* is more or less a walkover; *a facile remark* is a glib one, easy to make but not requiring much thought.

◦◕◙◦

fallacious

In logic a *fallacy* is an error of reasoning that produces a misleading conclusion; *fallacious* therefore means illogical, misleading, as in *a fallacious argument* or *a fallacious news report*. It's also worth being aware of what philosophers call *the fallacy of many questions*, of which 'When did you stop beating your wife?' is the most frequently given example. It means that the question presupposes something that may be false, but you can't answer it without acknowledging the accusation. Lose-lose.

◦◕◙◦

fastidious

This means picky, critical, hard to please and the Latin roots conjure up its connotations beautifully: they are the words for pride and weariness (the second part of *fastidious* is related to *tedious* and *tedium*). So the fastidious person looks down on something as being beneath her and manages to be bored with it at the same time. You might *pick fastidiously at your food* if it didn't appeal to you or *lift your trouser legs fastidiously* so as not to get them wet on a rainy day. Whatever the action, a sneer of disdain or a shiver of distaste is never far away.

◯◠◞◠◯

fatuous

Silly, empty-headed: 'If you have nothing better to do than to sit there making *fatuous* comments, you can help me set the table.' The nature of a clown may be considered *fatuous*, which, while sounding a bit mean to the clown, is probably what makes for an entertaining act.

◯◠◞◠◯

feckless

The noun *feck*, meaning the greater part or the substance of something, is obsolete except in regional/dialectical use; so too is the adjective *feckful* – effective or vigorous. But the adjective describing *a lack of feck*, and therefore meaning weak, ineffective and irresponsible, is alive and well. It's usually used – decidedly disapprovingly – of a person who can't be bothered to hold down a job or save for his/her retirement; such a person may be described as *feckless* or accused of having *feckless habits* or *a feckless lifestyle*. The resemblance to the chiefly Irish pronunciation of a similar but much ruder word is a happy coincidence.

fickle

The title of the aria 'La donna è mobile', from Verdi's opera *Rigoletto*, is usually translated as 'Woman is fickle' and George Bernard Shaw's play *The Philanderer* contains the heartfelt complaint, 'The fickleness of the women I love is only equalled by the infernal constancy of the women who love me.' The word comes from the Old English for deceitful and is applied to those who are inconstant in their affections – almost always, for some reason, women, although neither the (male) singer in *Rigoletto* nor the (also male) title character in *The Philanderer* is a model of chastity or fidelity. It can also be applied to other things that are unreliable: the weather, for example, or the fortune that may or may not favour you in a poker game.

flagrant

From the Latin for burning, this means very much the same as BLATANT – open and shameless. You can have *a flagrant breach of the rules* or *a flagrant disregard for Health and Safety regulations.* Also, of course, you can be caught *in flagrante delicto* (literally 'with the crime blazing' and often abbreviated to *in flagrante*) meaning 'in the act', usually with your hands in the till or your trousers round your ankles.

flout

As in *to flout authority*, this means to show contempt for and is nothing to do with *flounce*. That said, if you were *flouting your parents' authority* you might well *flounce out of the room*, leaving it in an obviously angry way and possibly slamming the door. Neither word has anything to do with *flaunt*, which means to display ostentatiously, even brazenly: 'Society was scandalized when he *flaunted* his latest mistress at the opera.' Flaunting doesn't have to be shocking, though; you could equally well *flaunt your new Porsche* at the school gates or *flaunt a designer dress* at a colleague's barbecue.

⚖

fulsome

Another much misused word, *fulsome* is *not* a synonym for enthusiastic. Only the most desperate want to receive *fulsome praise* or *fulsome compliments*: these are excessive, insincere and likely to be turned into snide backbiting the moment you are out of earshot. The word comes from a combination of *full* and *some* and originally meant abundant or plentiful, but acquired negative connotations quite early on in its career.

⚖

gourmand

This is the French for greedy and the last syllable is pronounced *mon* – the *d* is sounded only in the feminine form, *gourmande*. It is not a flattering word and should be clearly distinguished from *gourmet* (second syllable pronounced *may*), which means someone who is well-informed and discerning about food and wine. It is possible to be a *gourmet* without being a *gourmand* and vice versa, but all too easy to be both.

⚖

gratuitous

Unnecessary, uncalled for, as in *a gratuitous insult* or *a gratuitous sex scene.* Not to be confused with *gratuity*, which means a tip (in the financial sense, something you might give a waiter or a taxi driver) or *gratis*, which means free, for nothing: 'They were handing out the tickets *gratis*, but I still didn't want to go.'

❧

grotesque

A combination of distorted, distasteful and bizarre: 'It's *grotesque* to say that being a stay-at-home parent means you are sponging off society' or 'I had to turn off the wildlife film: those beetles with the bulging eyes were *grotesque*' or 'The feathers in that hat made her look positively *grotesque*.' In architectural terms, *grotesques* – odd mixtures of human and animal forms – are often carved on the side of cathedrals and the like; they become *gargoyles* only if they are designed to spout water.

❧

harangue

Pronounce this with the emphasis on the second syllable and as if the *–ue* wasn't there. It can be either a noun or a verb and means a lecture-like speech, a telling-off, or to make such a speech. Not as violent as a DIATRIBE and not necessarily offensively DIDACTIC, it is still lengthy and opinionated: 'He tries to *harangue* me on the subject of my clothes, but I just leave the room.' A *harangue* can also be loud and public: 'I like going to political rallies to listen to the candidates *haranguing* the crowd.'

❧

harridan

A polite word for an old bag, a bossy or nagging woman of (at best) a certain age: 'My geography teacher was a real *harridan*: no one ever dared hand their homework in late.'

◦◉✑◉

hirsute

Hairy, but in a shaggy and unkempt sort of way: it comes from the Latin for bristly. This nineteenth-century example gives the tone: 'Wearing his hair and beard unshorn … this *hirsute* and savage corsair seemed an embodiment of vengeance.' If you described someone as hirsute today you would be either disapproving or joking, or possibly both; it's not an adjective you would apply to the long, silky tresses seen in shampoo advertisements.

◦◉✑◉

histrionic

Showy, over-dramatic and insincere, most frequently applied to gestures: clasping your hands to your bosom to indicate shock could be described as *a histrionic gesture*, as could giving a large sum of money to charity and making sure the world knew about it. In either case, a critic might tell you that he had had enough of your *histrionics*.

◦◉✑◉

ignoble

In front of a word beginning with *n*, the prefix *ig-* means 'not', so *ignoble* is simply 'not noble'. For such a lowly word it has a rather grand sound to it, as in 'Far from the madding crowd's *ignoble* strife' (from Thomas Gray's 'Elegy Written in a Country Churchyard') and Milton's *Paradise Lost*, in which Belial is a demon:

Thus Belial with words cloth'd in reason's garb
Counselled *ignoble* ease, and peaceful sloth.

꧁≋꧂

ignominious

Another *ig-* word (see previous entry); the *nomin* part
comes from the Latin for name or reputation, so *ignominy*
means shame, disgrace or loss of reputation. Towards the
end of Shakespeare's *Henry IV, Part I*, Prince Hal, having
killed the brave young rebel Hotspur, remembers his rival's
many admirable qualities when he says:

Adieu, and take thy praise with thee to heaven!
Thy *ignominy* sleep with thee in the grave ...

In other words, let's forget that you did anything as
ignominious as revolt against the king. In modern use,
ignominious is not often applied to a person: it is more
likely to appear in a phrase such as *an ignominious act* or
an ignominious thought (one of which you are privately
ashamed: 'She was usually so exquisitely dressed that
I couldn't help feeling pleased to have caught her in
gardening clothes').

꧁≋꧂

ignoramus

From the Latin meaning 'we don't know', this is a
contemptuous word for an ignorant, ill-informed person:
'The man who interviewed me was a complete *ignoramus* –
the moment I started asking about the technical side of the
job, he was lost.'

꧁≋꧂

imprecation

An expletive, wishing ill on someone or something. It
is often used to mean no more than a swear word – 'He
uttered violent *imprecations* when the police came to
arrest him' – but strictly this would suggest he was hoping
the officers would die and go to hell rather than simply
shouting abuse at them. See also PROFANE.

incarnate

Born, 'made flesh' as in *the devil incarnate* – the devil,
alive and well and walking the Earth. It may also mean the
living embodiment of something unpleasant: *he is cruelty
incarnate*, he is really cruel, you can't imagine anything
crueller.

indolent

The original meaning is 'not feeling pain', but *indolent* has
come to signify simply lazy, unwilling to make an effort.
An indolent person is one who lounges on the sofa reading
a magazine and possibly eating snacks while there are
chores to be done.

iniquitous

A combination of wicked and unjust. It's a word to be
spoken with venom – if you think something is *iniquitous*,
you disapprove very strongly indeed: 'The way the
company treated the people who were being made
redundant was *iniquitous* – they had two weeks' notice and
only the legal minimum pay-off.' The noun is *iniquity*, and
it's every bit as bad.

insinuate

Derived from the Latin for curve, this means either to wind or worm your way into something – 'By helping her carry her shopping to the car I *insinuated* myself into her good graces' – or subtly and indirectly to suggest something unpleasant: 'He never accused her directly, but he *insinuated* enough to make her suspect he knew the truth.'

One of the methods you can use to insinuate something in this latter sense is *innuendo*. This odd-looking form is a Latin gerund or verbal noun and it derives from the word for 'to convey with a nod'. A nod's as good as a wink, in other words, nudge, nudge.

❦

insipid

Of a person, feeble, unable to stand up for themselves, generally uninteresting; of food, art, music and the like, dull, lacking in any appealing feature. As in: 'She's so *insipid* there's no point in asking her opinion; I've never heard her say anything remotely interesting' or 'Why is this soup so *insipid*? Didn't you have any onions?' or 'Sung with vigour it's a great anthem, but that version is completely *insipid.*'

❦

insouciant

Being *insouciant* isn't a very serious failing: it means carefree, unconcerned, but it does imply a lack of interest in other people's feelings or in the implications of your own actions. It might be applied to someone whose response to a world crisis would be to shrug her shoulders and casually wave her cigarette holder, possibly while holding a dry Martini in the other hand. The noun to sum this all up is *insouciance*, and both words should be pronounced with a suspicion of a French accent.

◦≋◦

insubordinate

Not having or displaying the qualities of a *subordinate*; thus, disrespectful or disobedient of one in authority. It would be *insubordinate* of a soldier not to salute a senior officer or of a junior employee to ignore company policy in dealing with clients. In natural history a *subordinate* member of a group (of wolves, perhaps) is submissive to the dominant one; in grammar a *subordinate* clause is dependent on the main clause and doesn't constitute a sentence in its own right.

◦≋◦

invidious

From the Latin for envy, this means both 'not likely to inspire envy' ('It is my *invidious* task to tell you that there will be no Christmas bonus this year', meaning that this is a task no one else would want to undertake) and 'making an unfair distinction' ('It is *invidious* to blame the majority of hard-working lawyers for the greediness of a few').

Invidious is not to be confused with *insidious*, which means stealthy, having a tendency to sneak up and then do something bad: *an insidious illness* is one whose early symptoms are difficult to detect, while *an insidious computer virus* will have eaten your hard drive before you realize it's there.

◦≋◦

kitsch

Tasteless, pretentious, excessively garish furniture, décor, etc., often harking back to an earlier time or mimicking something more classy in an attempt to appeal to popular taste. The word can be either an adjective or a noun, so you might find *kitsch crocheted tablecloths* in a *kitsch tea shop* whose décor was *the height of kitsch.*

libidinous

With the stress placed on the second syllable in both words, the *libido* is the energy released by sexual desire and to be *libidinous* is to feel that desire – particularly in an immoderate way. You can be a *libidinous person* (if you must) or feel *libidinous desires* or *libidinous urges* – it all boils down to the same thing.

louche

Another French word, pronounced to rhyme with *whoosh*. The English–French dictionary offers 'shady, shifty, dubious, suspicious, fishy' as translations, and *louche* tends to be used to describe the sort of person who turns up the collar of his trench coat and offers you black-market goods for which you, obviously, pay in cash.

lubricious

Another word for *lewd, lascivious* or indeed LIBIDINOUS, though this is more formal than any of them. It's from the same Latin root as *lubricate* and *lubricant*, with their implications of slipperiness and reducing friction. Enough said, don't you think?

magisterial

The Latin word that gave us *magistrate* actually means a schoolteacher, and *magisterial* means 'in the manner of a schoolteacher', but in the worst way – domineering and laying down the law.

❧

malignant

A nasty word, this – it means harmful, but with an unpleasant twist. *A malignant cancer* spreads rapidly and doesn't respond to treatment; *a malignant person* or *action* deliberately sets out to cause pain or unpleasantness. Think Shakespeare's Richard III or, if you prefer, Jafar in Disney's *Aladdin*, positively revelling in their own evil. The opposite of malignant in this sense is *benign* – kindly and generally well-disposed towards your fellow human beings. *Benignant* does exist but is rarer and often implies condescension, as in the way a gracious monarch behaves to his or her subjects.

❧

martinet

Not to be confused with *marionette*, which is a puppet moved by strings, a *martinet* is a strict disciplinarian. The word was originally used in a military context, but may now also apply to a teacher, a boss or even a particularly severe parent. Although it comes from the name of a French general, we pronounce it English-style, sounding the final *t*.

❧

mercenary

From the Latin for wages, this is all about money: as a noun, it refers to the sort of soldier who will fight on behalf of anyone if the price is right; as an adjective, it means influenced by the desire for (usually financial) gain. *A mercenary person* might want to marry somebody wealthy and could therefore be said to have *mercenary ambitions,* while *a mercenary writer* would churn out LUCRATIVE potboilers rather than applying her talents to a work of greater merit.

meretricious

Nothing to do with *merit* (you might be thinking of *meritorious*); this is right at the other end of the scale. It means flashy, gaudy, superficially attractive but, underneath all that, cheap. It can be used either literally (*meretricious jewellery* is bling by any other name) or figuratively (*a meretricious argument* would be plausible but false). *Meretricious* derives from the Latin for a prostitute, which in turn comes from the word for to hire. See also SPECIOUS.

narcissistic

In Greek mythology Narcissus was a beautiful but extraordinarily vain youth who fell in love with his own reflection in a pool and pined away, eventually being turned into the daffodil-like flower that is named after him. Not all *narcissism* leads to this drastic end, but it does make you unattractively self-obsessed. As the American journalist Jeffrey Kluger warned: 'It's a deep and all but certain truth about *narcissistic* personalities that to meet them is to love them, but to know them well is to find them unbearable. Confidence quickly curdles into arrogance; smarts turn to smugness, charm turns to smarm.'

⌒⬭⌒

noisome

Nothing to do with noise, this means harmful or objectionable and is usually applied to smells. The stench itself could be described as *noisome* or it might emanate from *a noisome apartment* in *a noisome slum*.

⌒⬭⌒

nugatory

Of little value or importance: 'He was there for three hours but made only a *nugatory* contribution to the work.' From a Latin word meaning to trifle; nothing to do with *nuggets*.

⌒⬭⌒

obsequious

Usually used of a servant or underling, this means obedient and attentive, but in a grovelling, overeager-to-please manner. Depending on your literary tastes, you could think of Uriah Heep in *David Copperfield* or Dobby in *Harry Potter*, though that is perhaps a bit harsh on Dobby, who grovels because he is a put-upon elf rather than because he is a creep. Uriah, on the other hand, is creepy to the marrow. And what's the difference between obsequiousness and sycophancy? The SYCOPHANT uses flattery; the obsequious person abases himself and invites you to walk all over him (or her, although this does tend – in literature at least – to be a male characteristic). In other words, the one boosts your ego, the other diminishes his own. Either of them is likely to turn your head if you aren't careful.

obstreperous

The word from which the slang *stroppy* is derived, this means noisy, unruly, resistant to discipline: 'He objected *obstreperously* to any suggestion that he might tidy his room' or 'An *obstreperous* crowd gathered outside the city, prepared to march on it and make the king surrender.'

odious

Another word for 'hateful'. A person you really dislike could be described as *odious*, as could their behaviour. The noun *odium* is rather literary and sounds most natural when applied to a stance taken by a public figure or to an institution: you might feel *odium* for a pro-war campaign or for a corrupt police force; it wouldn't be the right word to describe your attitude to a philandering ex-boyfriend (that would be hatred, pure and simple).

officious

Not the same thing as *official*, though *officials* and *officialdom* can certainly be *officious*. It means they butt in, giving advice or offering help when neither is necessary. *An officious enquiry* into your living arrangements would not only ask how many bedrooms you had but suggest how you might decorate them differently or question who you were sharing them with.

ostentatious

Showy. It's often tempting to call something *vulgarly ostentatious*, because it sounds so good, but in fact this is a TAUTOLOGY – *ostentation* is by definition vulgar, by virtue of lacking good taste and modesty.

palaver

A lot of talk or fuss about not very much: 'I can't stand those committee meetings – the chairman has no control over anything and it all ends in *palaver* and chaos'; or 'All that *palaver* about her health and it turns out she was sick because she'd eaten too many blackberries.'

parsimonious

If being FRUGAL can just about be passed off as a virtue (unless you are on the receiving end of the frugality), there is no such excuse for *parsimony*. Parsimonious people are downright mean; like Scrooge in Dickens' *A Christmas Carol,* they're prepared to put up with considerable discomfort themselves in order to save money. With a frugal person, you might think twice about whether or not you wanted to stay at their place for the weekend; with a parsimonious one it wouldn't be a problem because you wouldn't be asked.

pathological

Pathology is the study of disease and *pathological* is the adjective derived from it: *a pathological fear of flying* would be considered a medical disorder rather than wimpishness. Away from the medical world, however, we use it casually to describe something we can't help doing, which we do compulsively and habitually. The most common use is in the expression *a pathological liar*, but Bill Bryson gives a slight twist in his book *One Summer: America 1927* – one of aviation's pioneering entrepreneurs apparently had 'a *pathological* inability to be frank with anyone' and 'seemed sometimes to be lying simply for the sake of it'.

peccadillo

This is Spanish for 'little sin' and means just that: a small fault, almost too trivial to mention. It's often used as a EUPHEMISM for a man's unfaithfulness in marriage, with the implication that *these little peccadillos* are nothing for a wife to be upset about. A pre-feminist concept, you might say.

❧

pejorative

From the Latin for worse, this often describes a word that carries an unpleasant and disparaging connotation. In this section, for example, HIRSUTE is a pejorative word for hairy, suggesting that the speaker disapproves of the hairiness; TERMAGANT and VIRAGO are pejorative terms for a woman of strong character and opinions.

❧

peremptory

Brief to the point of brusqueness, expecting immediate obedience, as in *a peremptory command*. Not to be confused with *perfunctory*, which is also brief but means done superficially, carelessly or as a matter of routine: giving someone's hand *a perfunctory shake* would not make them feel welcome, while *a perfunctory glance at the headlines* would give you only a vague understanding of current affairs.

❧

perfidious

Treacherous, prone to going back on your word; the connected noun is *perfidy*. It's a powerful word: when in the 1830s it was proposed to remove the Cherokee people from the state of Georgia, the American philosopher Ralph Waldo Emerson wrote in protest to President Martin van Buren:

You, sir, will bring down that renowned chair in which
you sit into infamy if your seal is set to this instrument
of *perfidy*; and the name of this nation ... will stink to the
world.

You can't get much more damning than that.

❦

persiflage
From the French for teasing, this means light-hearted, good-
natured banter, or a flippant way of treating something: 'He
was a great one for *persiflage* when he was talking about
money, but it didn't alter the fact that he was heavily in debt.'

❦

petulant
Sulky, irritable and impatient, often used of adults who are
behaving childishly. '"Why won't you come?" "Because I
just won't," she replied *petulantly*.'

❦

philistine
In the Bible, the Philistines were a people living in
Palestine, enemies of the Israelites and regarded by them
as totally uncultured. In modern English, therefore, a
philistine is a combination of an IGNORAMUS and a boor
(see BOORISH). Philistines are not only ignorant, specifically
about the arts but more generally about good manners
and civilized behaviour, they are actively dismissive of
the importance of any of these things. 'There's no point
in taking him to the play: he's a complete *philistine*. If he
doesn't make rude remarks during the performance he'll
fall asleep and snore all the way through the second act.'

pugnacious

Ready for a fight; inclined to be affronted and throw the first punch. The word comes from the Latin for fight and is therefore strictly speaking less violent than *belligerent*, which comes from the word for war. You may have *a pugnacious* (or *belligerent*) *attitude to authority*; be prone to making *pugnacious* (or *belligerent*) *remarks* or simply be of *a pugnacious* (or *belligerent*) *disposition*. Not many people would bother making a distinction, but if there is one it is that *pugnacity* is a characteristic of an individual, unlikely to lead to anything worse than fisticuffs; *belligerence* could be shown by a gang or a nation and have a more serious outcome.

rampant

Used in heraldry (*lion rampant* or *dragon rampant*), this has the specific meaning of standing on the hind legs with the right foreleg raised above the left. If you're not talking about a coat of arms, it means unrestrained, flourishing unchecked. A garden may be taken over by *rampant weeds* or a political group infiltrated by *rampant activists*.

It shouldn't be confused with *rampage*, which means to rush violently about: an angry mob might *rampage through the streets*, no doubt smashing windows as they went, but not necessarily with their right forelegs raised above their left.

rankle

To allow something to *rankle* is to let it annoy you long after the event, to let it fester. 'It still *rankles* that she won "best in show" when my roses were so much more beautiful than hers.' This is an intransitive verb, so you can't *rankle someone* or *something*; the insult or hurt *rankles with you*.

❧

rapacious

Grasping, from the same root as the birds of prey known as *raptors*. The context is normally financial, where it is used of bankers, lawyers and others who have a reputation for getting hold of other people's money and hanging on tightly to it.

❧

reductionist

Reductionism is the act of reducing or analysing something complicated into simpler terms; this action is described as *reductionist* and the word can also be a noun applied to the person who does it. It's normally disparaging, carrying the accusation of over-simplification: *a reductionist attitude to the economic situation* or *a reductionist study of the perils of global warming*.

❧

risible

Deserving to be laughed at, as in *a risible attempt at tragedy* (with a script so bad it makes the audience laugh) or *a risible error in calculation* ($2 + 2 = 7$). Although this isn't obvious at first glance, the word comes from the same Latin root as *ridiculous*.

❧

rodomontade

Possibly the only word in the English language to derive from the name of a character in fifteenth-century Italian epic poetry. In *Orlando Innamorato* and *Orlando Furioso*, Rodomonte is a Saracen king, known for his blustering and bragging. *Rodomontade* can be either a noun – blustering and boastful behaviour or speech – or a verb meaning to talk in this way.

✎

scurrilous

Defamatory or abusive, often in the expression *a scurrilous report*. *Scurrilous jokes* can be funny, but are still insulting and/or obscene: Shakespeare in *The Winter's Tale* has an entertainer forewarned 'that he use no *scurrilous* words in his tunes'. The implication is that, left to himself, he might have been a bit bawdy.

✎

sententious

This is a degree worse than being MAGISTERIAL. Whereas the magisterial person is merely domineering, the *sententious* one is pompous, too. *Sententiousness* originally meant that your conversation was full of aphorisms – short, PITHY sayings – which might have been quite interesting, but the PEJORATIVE sense has largely taken over. If someone describes you or your writing as *sententious*, you shouldn't assume that they are praising your wit.

✎

skulduggery

This wonderful word sounds as if it should be reserved for the sort of rollicking piratical behaviour exhibited by Johnny Depp in *Pirates of the Caribbean*. Sadly, the dictionaries say it is of obscure origin and there is no reason to connect it either with skulls or with digging (for buried treasure or anything else); it actually means 'underhand behaviour or intrigue'. Inevitably, perhaps, in these cynical times, it is commonly preceded by either 'political' or 'financial'.

෧ৡৣ৩

specious

Plausible; appearing right or truthful but being nothing of the sort. *A specious argument* sounds good but doesn't stand up to analysis; *a specious claim to an inheritance* might be made by someone pretending to be a long-lost son. See also MERETRICIOUS.

෧ৡৣ৩

spurious

A *spurious* claim to an inheritance would be every bit as phoney as a SPECIOUS one (see previous entry) and wouldn't even have the advantage of appearing true. While *specious* is about appearances, *spurious* derives from a Latin word meaning of illegitimate birth, or illegitimate or false in other ways. A landlord might make *a spurious justification* for a rent increase (pretending that the maintenance costs were higher than they were); a fiancée might break off an engagement on the *spurious grounds* that she didn't feel ready for commitment (when in fact she was holding out for a richer man).

෧ৡৣ৩

stentorian

In Greek mythology Stentor was a herald with a particularly loud voice (useful in his line of business) and *stentorian* is applied to any noticeably loud voice or sound: Gilbert Gottfried and Patrick Stewart might express their views *in stentorian tones* or you might ring a doorbell *in a stentorian manner* if you were determined to be let in.

❦

stringent

Often applied to regulations, this means requiring strict attention to detail and procedure, allowing no scope for imagination or discretion. *Stringent laws* applied to gun control or immigration, for example, would mean that the rules were absolutely clear cut and had to be followed to the letter. *Stringent conditions* for entry to a university would mean that you had to get the grades – end of story.

❦

supererogation

More than is required, with the implication of officiousness (see OFFICIOUS): 'It was an act of *supererogation* for her to explain what I had to do, given that I've done it every day for the last six months.'

❦

sycophantic

Grovellingly flattering to someone with influence, hoping to win favour. 'Sir Walter Raleigh's putting his cloak over a muddy puddle for Queen Elizabeth I to walk on has often been described as a gallant gesture; am I alone in thinking it was nauseatingly *sycophantic*?' A remark as well as a gesture may be *sycophantic* – 'Oh, I do *so* agree with you, your lordship' – and the person who utters it is a *sycophant.*

❦

tawdry

Cheap and tatty, from the goods sold at medieval fairs in honour of St Audrey (split that as *sain taudrey* and it makes more sense). The word is used to describe various forms of adornment (*tawdry earrings*, *a tawdry substitute for velvet*) or emotion (*the tawdry sentimentality* of low-budget rom-coms).

ᦧ

termagant

Another term of abuse for a woman, this is noisier and more bad-tempered than a HARRIDAN. A harridan is merely a strict disciplinarian; a *termagant* is a scold, a nag and a shrew. In fact, the original Termagant was male: a violent and arrogant deity in medieval morality plays. That was still the case in Shakespeare's day: he doesn't use the word in *The Taming of the Shrew*, but in *Henry IV, Part I* he has Falstaff describe the hot-headed rebel Hotspur as 'that hot termagant Scot'. However, the female bias had become established by the late seventeenth century and remains to this day.

ᦧ

truculent

This means much the same as PUGNACIOUS: stroppy (see OBSTREPEROUS), defiant, always ready to disagree, though not necessarily to start throwing punches. Former US President Dwight D. Eisenhower summed it up nicely when he said, 'There is, in world affairs, a steady course to be followed between an assertion of strength that is *truculent* and a confession of helplessness that is cowardly.'

ᦧ

turpitude

'Moral turpitude' is the usual expression – it is a legal concept in the USA and describes behaviour that is contrary to accepted social norms, or to community standards of justice, honesty or good morals. Having a conviction for such a misdeed is enough to have a would-be immigrant turned back from American shores. Away from passport control, near synonyms include 'baseness' and 'depravity' – not attractive qualities.

The associated adjective appears in the OED online, but not in many single-volume dictionaries: a shame, because if ever there was a word that could be spat in the direction of someone you disliked it is surely *turpitudinous*. Say it out loud a few times and see if you don't agree that it is due for a revival.

unconscionable

Unscrupulous and immoderate, having no conscience: *an unconscionable rogue*, meaning a complete and utter rogue; *unconscionable demands*, shamelessly unreasonable ones. Not to be confused with *unconscious*, which means having no consciousness, unaware, not having the normal use of one's senses.

untoward

Unlucky, unfavourable or improper: a doctor may find *nothing untoward* as a result of taking your blood pressure, while you might also check the bedrooms during a teenager's party to check that *nothing untoward* was going on.

uxorious

You wouldn't think that being fond of your wife could be a bad thing, but a man who is described as *uxorious* is over-fond or overly dependent on her. It may be good to be happy at home by the fireside rather than being out, but the implication here is that you are getting in your wife's hair.

❧

vehement

Of opinions, strongly and intensely expressed; of a person, emphatic and forceful: 'Despite all the objections we raised, he was *vehement* in support of the proposal' or 'She denied the accusations *vehemently*.'

❧

virago

A TERMAGANT by any other name: a loud and angry woman, from an Old English term for a manlike female. *Vir* is the Latin for man and recurs in words such as *virile* and *virtue*; funnily enough, although the latter is now often used to mean chastity in a female, it comes from the Latin for manliness or courage.

❧

vituperative

Abusive, fault-finding, strongly and unkindly critical. *A vituperative argument* or *a vituperative divorce* would both be long, loud and full of ill-feeling.

❧

vociferous

Clamorous, loud, particularly in protest against something. *A vociferous group of demonstrators* might, for example, make *vociferous objections* (or *object vociferously*) to the latest government initiative.

〜〜

voracious

Greedy, though not exclusively for food. You can certainly have *a voracious appetite* – for food or for sex – but on a slightly calmer level you may also be *a voracious reader.* It has also been said that Hollywood has *a voracious appetite for new people* and the Chinese economy *a voracious demand for energy*, so on the whole *voracity* or *voraciousness* (both words exist, though the latter is more commonly used) is an excessive quality better kept in check. It's not to be confused with *veracious,* which means telling the truth, nor with its related noun *veracity*, truthfulness.

〜〜

wanton

This has both a sexual and a non-sexual sense. As an adjective it can mean promiscuous; it may also be a noun, meaning a promiscuous person, usually a woman. The seventeenth-century poet Anthony Munday wrote of coming across a beautiful woman bathing by a spring:

> My *wanton* thoughts enticed mine eye
> To see what was forbidden.

There's little doubt, I suggest, about what he means. Alternatively the word can mean wild and uncontrolled in other areas of life: *wanton extravagance,* for example, or *the wanton destruction of the rainforests*. Whichever way, it's disapproving.

CHAPTER THREE

It Depends on My Mood

This chapter is about feeling cheerful or miserable, interested or bored, affectionate or otherwise towards our fellow human beings. Whether we are being decisive or indecisive, bossy or subservient or simply out to have a good time, we always seem to have just the word to sum up the mood of the moment and to describe the personalities that go with it.

alacrity

This is a combination of liveliness, briskness and enthusiasm: you accept an invitation *with alacrity* when 1) you very much want to accept it and 2) you are afraid the inviter might change his or her mind. As in, '"I'd love to come in for coffee," he said with *alacrity*.'

❦

ambivalent

The prefix *ambi-* means 'both' or 'round, on both sides' – *ambidextrous*, skilled with both hands; *ambiguous*, having more than one possible meaning; *ambient*, relating to the immediate surroundings, as in *the ambient temperature*; even *ambience*, the atmosphere of a place. *Ambivalent* means having two conflicting opinions or feelings at the same time: *I am ambivalent about her* means 'I can't make up my mind whether I like her or not'; a government could be *ambivalent about reform*, because it knew it was a positive move (and might win votes), but also that it would be expensive.

❦

bacchanalian

Bacchus was the Roman god of wine, frequently portrayed as a fat, red-cheeked, elderly man who has obviously been having a lot of fun for a long time. (Oddly, he's also sometimes portrayed as a handsome youth or, alarmingly, as a very fat baby, stuffing his face with grapes.) Although a bunch of grapes is often strategically placed, he is almost always naked. The revels associated with the worship of Bacchus – *bacchanalia* – involved drink, partying and sex. In modern parlance, therefore, the word *bacchanalian* is most frequently followed by *orgy*, usually an exaggerated description of a wild party. Bacchus's counterpart in Greek mythology was Dionysus, and you are welcome to have *Dionysian* orgies if you prefer, though the word is less commonly used and, perhaps for that reason, usually spelled with a capital.

❦

blighting

A blighting remark or *a blighting response* is an unpleasant way of putting someone else in their place, to make them feel uncomfortable or stupid. It's connected with the plant disease *blight,* which in turn gives the figurative sense of 'She was a real *blight* on the evening' – she was so miserable no one else could enjoy themselves. *Being a blight* need not be intentional, whereas anyone making *a blighting remark* knows exactly what they are doing.

❦

bucolic

Not so much a passing mood as a general state of being: it refers to the countryside and country life, and gives the impression of slowness, being unspoiled and far from the urban scene. A novel might be described as having *a bucolic setting,* while someone who had quit the rat race and moved to the country might be living *a bucolic life.* That second example might be complimentary or it might be a little patronizing: while *bucolic* doesn't have to mean straw-chewingly idiotic, it would never be confused with sophisticated or hip. See URBANE for a complete contrast and BOORISH and CHURLISH for less pleasant variations on the theme.

❦

caustic

In school chemistry, sodium hydroxide was commonly known as *caustic soda* and it burned into anything it was spilled on. That's the literal meaning of this word, 'capable of burning or corroding', and outside the chemistry lab it means much the same: biting, sarcastic, cutting. *A caustic remark* is intended to hurt; if you are thin-skinned you might also be advised to steer clear of someone with *a caustic sense of fun*.

⌒≋⌒

chastened

This is how you might feel after someone had made a CAUSTIC remark (see previous entry): abashed, embarrassed and likely to be more subdued and careful in the future. A banking executive whose bank had recently lost £691 million described it as 'a *chastening* experience', which you would hope had a strong element of understatement in it. The word comes from the Latin and French for punishment, but nowadays you are more likely to be chastened by someone's withering tongue than by whips and lashes.

⌒≋⌒

congenial

A *genial* person is friendly and cheerful; add the Latin prefix *con-*, meaning 'with', and you have someone who is pleasant to be with, someone with similar attitudes and interests to you: you might describe such a person as *congenial company* and they might also create *a congenial atmosphere*. This isn't the same as *a convivial atmosphere*, which is equally enjoyable but tends to involve partying and drink. Nor has it anything to do with *congenital*, which is used to describe a disease or abnormal condition you were born with, such as *congenital deafness*.

〇〰〇

contrary

Pronounced as in the nursery rhyme (with the emphasis on the second syllable, so that it rhymes with 'Mary, Mary'), this means deliberately going against whatever has been suggested. *A contrary person* will insist on staying in when you would like to go out, not because they are tired or short of money but because they refuse on principle to do what you want. With the emphasis on the first syllable, *contrary* means opposing, as in *contrary to public opinion*. *Contra* is the Latin for 'against' and is found again in *contradiction* (speaking against someone else), *contraflow* (two lanes of traffic going against each other on the motorway), *contraindication* (an indication against something, such as taking a particular drug under certain adverse conditions) and many others.

〇〰〇

contrite

In the Christian Church an *Act of Contrition* is a prayer in which the sinner not only confesses and promises to do penance for past sins but resolves not to repeat them in the future. Away from the church context, to be contrite is to feel guilty, remorseful, truly sorry. You would offer *a contrite apology* when you had upset another person badly and were anxious to make amends.

〇〰〇

demeanour

The outward display of feelings or mood, the way you behave. For example, 'She looked very cheerful: there was nothing in her *demeanour* to show that she was upset' or 'If I'm feeling confident, it shows in my *demeanour* – I stand taller, hold my stomach in and don't need to grit my teeth.' The word is connected to *misdemeanour*, a minor crime or piece of bad behaviour, but *to demean*, to lower oneself or to humble someone else, comes from a different root.

disingenuous

Not to be confused with *ingenious*, which means inventive, 'thinking outside the box', *disingenuous* means insincere while making a claim of sincerity. 'I didn't think you cared about Valentine's Day' might be *a disingenuous remark* from someone who had forgotten, or not bothered, to send a card.

dispassionate

The *dis-* prefix suggests negativity, so *dispassionate* is clearly not passionate. But it's actually a more positive quality than that. It means not *influenced* by passion and therefore impartial, unbiased: a good thing for, say, a judge to be. You might also be *a dispassionate observer* of an emotional situation in which you were not involved.

dispirited

Having lost spirit and therefore cast down, discouraged. 'I was enthusiastic at first, but their cool response has made me feel a bit *dispirited*.'

distraught

This is closely related to *distract*, meaning to draw the attention away from but also to bewilder or perplex. One meaning of *distracted* is deeply troubled: you can be *distracted with worry* or some other strong emotion. *Distraught* can similarly be followed by *with worry* or *with fear*, or you may simply be *distraught,* with the cause of your trouble unspecified but still distressing.

dolorous

The musical instruction *doloroso* means the piece is to be played mournfully; if such music affected you deeply you might have *a dolorous expression* on your face or even be reduced to *weeping dolorously*. It's a rather fancy word in modern English, so you should probably use it in either a literary context or a jokey one.

forlorn

He went like one that hath been stunned,
And is of sense *forlorn*:
A sadder and a wiser man,
He rose the morrow morn ...

... wrote Samuel Taylor Coleridge of the wedding guest at the end of *The Rime of the Ancient Mariner.* He meant that the poor man had had his senses wrenched from him, he was bereft, abandoned and miserable. The word is most commonly used in the expression *a forlorn hope*, one that is unlikely to be fulfilled, but an abandoned dog at the side of the road could also be described as *forlorn* and would almost certainly be wearing *a forlorn expression*. It's a sad, lonely word, in need of comfort.

gargantuan

From a fictional giant created by the sixteenth-century French satirist Rabelais, this means huge and is often applied to appetites of all kinds: *a gargantuan appetite* could equally well mean an enthusiasm for life, sex or chocolate. See also RABELAISIAN.

❧

hapless

Hap is an archaic word for luck or chance, related to both *happy* and *happen*. To be *hapless*, then, is to be unfortunate, a victim of an unkind fate or of circumstances beyond your control. A minor central Asian state could be described as *a hapless victim of Genghis Khan's marauding* or the smallest child in the playground *the hapless focus of the bully's attention*.

❧

immutable

Unchangeable, but in a firm, digging-in-the-heels sense: *the immutable laws of the universe* or *the immutable doctrine of the survival of the fittest*.

❧

imperious

To do with *empire* and *imperial,* this means bossy and high-handed, giving orders in a way that assumes they will be obeyed: '"Get out of my way," he said *imperiously* (or 'with an *imperious* wave of the hand')'. Not to be confused with *impervious*, which means unable to be penetrated – either literally by, say, water (you might use *an impervious membrane* to line a pond), or metaphorically by what is said to you: 'His determination to have his own way made him *impervious* to abuse, persuasion or tears.'

impetuous

The Ancient Greek historian Thucydides wrote that 'few things are brought to a successful issue by *impetuous* desire, but most by calm and prudent forethought', and he may well have been right. Meaning acting hastily, without sufficient thought, this is not as unreliable as CAPRICIOUS, but still comes firmly under the heading of 'fools rush in'. A person, an action, a decision, a departure may all be *impetuous*. *Impetus*, meaning momentum, something that propels us onwards, has a similar derivation.

implicit

In one of its senses, this is the opposite of *explicit* – implied, not spelled out, but there nonetheless – 'He didn't lose his temper, but the *implicit* anger in his voice left me in no doubt that I was in trouble.' *Implicit* also means complete, absolute, as in 'I have *implicit* trust in your judgement; I'll do whatever you think is best.'

incandescent

Glowing with heat, emitting light specifically because your temperature has been raised; in a literal sense it's applied to certain sorts of lighting, such as *incandescent bulbs*. Figuratively, the most frequently heard image is *incandescent with rage* – absolutely white hot with it. The adjective can be used as a compliment, though: it's often applied to the actor Cate Blanchett, whose talent means she glows from the stage or screen.

indifferent

'It's a matter of complete *indifference* to me' is a posh way of saying, 'I don't care.' You can be *indifferent* to a person, a place, a food, a film – you neither like nor dislike them and when the chips are down you can't really be bothered to discuss them.

inexorable

The *or* in the middle of this word comes from the Latin for to pray or plead and is connected with *oratory* and *oration*. *Exorable* – which is found in dictionaries but not often used – means able to be moved by pleading and *inexorable* is the opposite. It is usually applied to something like a decline or a progression: 'the *inexorable* rise in food prices', 'her *inexorable* descent into dementia'. 'Relentless' would often do instead, but there is perhaps something even more relentless about being *inexorable*.

innate

Inborn, instinctive, an essential part of a person's character. It's usually used of a positive quality: 'His *innate* good manners helped him to deal with even the oddest situations' or 'He had an *innate* understanding of the sport, even though he had never played it.' The word comes from the Latin for born and is connected to *natal*, pertaining to birth, and related conditions such as *antenatal care* and *postnatal depression*; from the same root come *nativity* (specifically Christ's birth), *nature* and *natural*.

inveterate

Long-established, ingrained, confirmed as a habit, usually a bad one: *an inveterate smoker* has been doing it for years and is unlikely to give up now. 'They are *inveterate tourists*' doesn't just mean that they are always away but implies a certain disapproval – they may be avoiding the responsibilities they would have to face if they stayed at home. The middle part of the word comes from the Latin for old and is related to *veteran*, someone who has fought in a certain war (*a Vietnam veteran*) or seen long service in their occupation (*a veteran actor* celebrating fifty years in cinema).

❧

lachrymose

One step worse than DOLOROUS: you have gone beyond being sorrowful and have been reduced to tears. It's not a sympathetic word, this: if someone describes you as being in *a lachrymose condition* they mean you are giving in to your emotions and weeping all over the place. See also MAUDLIN.

❧

laconic

Laconia was the province of Ancient Greece whose capital was Sparta and its people were famous for the terseness of their speech. The story goes that Philip of Macedon, having conquered other parts of Greece, sent a message, 'If I enter Laconia, I shall raze Sparta to the ground.' In reply, he received the single word 'If.' It's a perfect example of *laconic* speech: brief, to the point, laid back, with just a touch of wit.

❧

lambent

From the Latin for *to lick*, this literally describes a flame
flickering gently over a surface, or figuratively something
else that glows gently. You can turn *a lambent gaze* on
someone, but only if you have particularly beautiful and
expressive eyes.

manifest

Obvious, easy to see. A buxom woman might be described
as having *manifest attractions*; or it might be said of an
underrated artist that time would *make manifest* his great
talent. A *manifestation* can mean a show, a demonstration,
as in, 'We all resigned as a *manifestation* of loyalty after she
was sacked'; or it can be the appearance of a spirit – the
early scenes of *Hamlet* include the *manifestation* of the
ghost of the dead king. A *manifesto*, from an Italian form
of the same word, is – in theory – an open, easy-to-see
declaration of a political party's policies.

maudlin

Over-sentimental, possibly even LACHRYMOSE. A person,
a condition, a remark or even a play or film may all be
maudlin, but the word isn't a compliment to any of them.
It's often used to describe the condition otherwise referred
to as 'tired and emotional' – that is, induced by drink.

maverick

If you're raising cattle on a ranch in North America, a
maverick is a calf you haven't branded yet; if it wanders
off you're unlikely to get it back because no one will know

it belongs to you. If a person is a *maverick*, he or she has a tendency to stray from the beaten path, normally in the sense of not holding orthodox views and being independent-minded. *A maverick politician*, for example, isn't one who willingly toes the party line.

◦◦◦

memorabilia

Related to *memory*, these are objects that help you to remember a person or event. Coronation mugs may be *royal memorabilia*; and almost anything from war medals to concert tickets can be described as *memorabilia* if you don't want to call them souvenirs or junk.

◦◦◦

mercurial

Mercury was the messenger of the Roman gods; he flitted about with a winged helmet and sandals and was also the god of eloquence, skill, trade and theft. The metal that is named after him is the only one that is liquid at room temperature, so it too has a tendency to flit about. A *mercurial* person or temperament can therefore be lively and quick-witted but changeable and unpredictable. More fun than a CAPRICIOUS one, but still not entirely to be relied upon.

◦◦◦

misanthropist

The derivation here is the Greek *anthropos,* meaning a human, which also crops up in *anthropology, anthropoid apes* and various other scientific contexts. A *misanthropist,* therefore, dislikes the entire human race. Less all-encompassing terms are *misandrist*, someone who hates only the male sex, and *misogynist*, whose objection is to women.

obdurate

The *dur* here relates to hardness and is connected with *durable* and *enduring*. An *obdurate* person is hard-hearted, obstinate, unlikely to be moved by persuasion. Much the same as INEXORABLE, in fact, except that obdurate is usually applied to a person rather than to a relentless force.

obeisance

This comes from the French for obey, but it doesn't mean *obedience*. It is either a gesture or an attitude of deferential respect, such as a bow – 'They made *obeisance* to the statue before leaving the temple' – or an acknowledgement of someone or something's superior status – 'He wore evening dress as an *obeisance* to the formality of the occasion.'

pique

Often *a fit of pique*, a feeling of resentment or of having your pride wounded. 'She was normally quite happy to go to his mother's for dinner, but refused out of *pique* when he said his mother was a better cook than she was.' Confusingly, you can also *pique yourself* – in a perfectly pleasant, unboastful way – on doing something well, taking pride in your ability: 'She had always *piqued herself* on producing a good meal, so his remark was particularly hurtful.' See also PIQUANT.

plaintive

Often used of a voice or a piece of music, this means sorrowful, melancholy: '"I can't go to sleep," said a *plaintive* voice when I went to check on the children' or, towards, the end of Keats' 'Ode to a Nightingale', 'Adieu! Adieu! thy *plaintive* anthem fades.' This isn't to be confused with a *plaintiff*, who is the person who brings a civil action in a court of law (as opposed to the *defendant*, the person they bring the action against).

❦

poignant

Pronounced (approximately) *poin-yant*, this ultimately comes from the same Latin root as PUNGENT, but has been diverted via French. It means piercing in the sense of something that is particularly cutting, that pierces your heart emotionally. A *poignant* remark, song or poem will make you feel sad without necessarily bringing back any personal memories, while a visit to a graveyard may be *poignant* in its reminders of lives lost.

❦

polemical

Controversial, particularly when concerned with a belief or doctrine: a blogger who expressed opinions about world affairs rather than writing about personal matters could be described as *polemical* and a piece of his writing might be a *polemic*. Polemics are very often *against* something: 'a heartfelt *polemic* against the nationalization of railways' or '… against the government's healthcare policy'. To earn the description of a polemic – as opposed to, say, a DIATRIBE or a HARANGUE – the writing or speech needs to be passionate, but also well-reasoned and persuasive.

❦

pragmatic

Making a decision based on the prevailing circumstances rather than a philosophical or idealistic one: 'In an ideal world, we would rewrite the whole script, but as we have a deadline to meet we need a more *pragmatic* approach – how much of this can we live with?'

predilection

A near-synonym for *preference*, with the suggestion of INNATE bias or of having made up your mind in advance. You can have a *predilection* for almost anything from poetry to bright clothes, from cheese on toast to camping holidays – it's simply a thing that you like, have always liked and will probably continue to like for the rest of your days. Take note of the spelling of this word; it's an easy one to get wrong.

propensity

An inclination or tendency: 'He has a *propensity* to tell you his life story at every opportunity' or 'If your family has a *propensity* towards high cholesterol, it is worth having yours checked.'

prostrate

Prostrate means lying flat on the floor, face down, usually in submission: you might in olden times have been expected to *prostrate yourself* before your emperor, if you happened to have one. The word can also be used to describe emotions: you might be *prostrate with* (or *prostrated by*) *grief* or *overwork*, but you run the risk of sounding melodramatic if you say so yourself. See also SUPINE. This is not to be confused with the gland that causes elderly men trouble: the *prostate*.

❧

querulous

Like PLAINTIVE, but less sympathetic: *a querulous tone* is whining and irritable. The OED quotes an eighteenth-century sermon describing 'a People always *querulous* and complaining, very prone to Lamentations and Wailings'. Not ideal party guests, in other words.

❧

quiescent

Associated with *quiet* and from the Latin for 'to rest', this means inactive, willing to go along with things without fuss. It's often used in politics (*the normally quiescent voters of the south-east*) and in science (*the quiescent phase of a disease*), though it's also possible to catch a normally difficult person in *a quiescent mood*.

❧

Rabelaisian

François Rabelais (*c.* 1483–1553) was the French satirist who created Gargantua (see GARGANTUAN). His works are bawdy and earthy, full of farting, over-eating and broad comedy, and that is what the adjective derived from his name means.

❧

rambunctious

Often mistakenly pronounced *rumbunctious*, this is a jocular word for boisterous, noisily enthusiastic, but also determined and uncompromising. It's an adult quality, though: you are more likely to have *a rambunctious political rally* or even *a rambunctious sex life* than *a rambunctious children's party*, however boisterous the latter might be.

❧

reminiscent

Evoking memories of something else: 'The scent of roses was *reminiscent* of that garden in Paris'; 'The show was *reminiscent* of a cheesy Seventies sitcom.' *Reminiscences* are memories of one's past: 'I love listening to Grandma's *reminiscences* (or 'when Grandma *reminisces*') – she obviously had a great time when she was my age.'

❧

ribald

'I never quibbled if it was ribald,' sang the satirist Tom Lehrer in his song 'Smut', and *ribaldry* is never far removed from smuttiness. The difference, perhaps, is that smut tends to be mildly offensive whereas ribaldry is rather fun. 'Disrespectfully amusing' is one neat definition, as in a *ribald remark* or a *ribald joke.*

❧

sangfroid

This is French for 'cold blood' but it doesn't mean *cold-blooded* in the English sense. It's a noun, so you would do something *with sangfroid*, carrying it off with style and verve. Perhaps the nearest English equivalents are 'composure' or 'self-possession', but both lack those other excellent Gallic qualities *panache* and *élan*.

❧

sanguine

This is also to do with blood, but refers back to the ancient belief in the four primary fluids in the body – phlegm, choler, melancholy and blood. Your 'dominant' fluid determined what sort of person you were: you could be *phlegmatic* – unexcitable; *choleric* – quick to anger; *melancholic* – sad and thoughtful; or *sanguine*. Medicine has moved on since this theory prevailed, but having *a sanguine disposition* still means being cheerful, optimistic, confident and possibly also of a ruddy complexion, denoting that you have plenty of blood in your veins. And arteries. Although melancholy was associated with bile (which we now know is secreted by the gall bladder), in ancient times it was also linked to the spleen, from which we derive the splendid adjective *splenetic*, meaning bad-tempered, impatient and spiteful.

sensibility

If you've read or seen Jane Austen, you should know exactly what this means; if not, the key is not to confuse it with sensibleness. *Sensibility* is almost exactly the opposite of sensibleness: it means responding with the senses or the emotions rather than the brain, and often to excess. A self-styled *person of exquisite sensibility* is almost certainly a pain in the neck: he likes to think he is extremely sensitive, in an interesting way, but in fact makes a fuss if the clock ticks too loudly or there is a hint of dust on the mantelpiece. On the other hand, you should be careful not to wound other people's *sensibilities* – in the plural and in a context like that it just means feelings. The adjective deriving from this is, confusingly, *sensible* ('I am deeply *sensible* of your generosity'), but it may be better to avoid it and use *aware*, *grateful* or *sensitive*, as appropriate.

soporific

Like the lettuce in *Peter Rabbit* or a particularly long and boring play – likely to send you to sleep. It can be neutral or complimentary – an insomniac, for example, would probably be glad of *a soporific drug* – but can also be mildly insulting: no composer wants to be told that his music is soporific. Iris Murdoch's novel *The Sandcastle* featured perhaps the most damning use ever: she referred to one character as beginning to have *a soporific feeling of conjugal boredom*. May the fates preserve us all from being stuck in that sort of relationship.

❦

subservient

If to be *subordinate* (see INSUBORDINATE) is to know that you are of lesser importance, recognizing your place in the pecking order, being *subservient* is putting yourself a step further down the scale. Referring to an object or a policy, it can simply mean 'less important than'. 'If she wanted to win an Olympic medal, all other considerations had to be *subservient* to her training.' But of a person there is likely to be a sense of grovelling, of acting inferior: if you were to say, for example, 'He stood in a *subservient* attitude while the manager conducted her inspection', you'd expect him to be holding his cap and possibly tugging his forelock.

❦

supine

Perhaps more a physical position than an indication of mood, *supine* literally means lying on one's back (as opposed to PROSTRATE or *prone*, lying on one's front). But the word sneaks into this section because it can also mean indolent, inactive and apathetic. If you are *prostrate with exhaustion* and *prone to migraine* you may reasonably expect people may feel sorry for you; if you are *supine* or *supinely acquiescent* it is your own fault and you are likely to be told to pick yourself up and get on with it.

❦

tenacious

'Holding on to', in the sense of being persistent or stubborn – 'The detective's questioning was *tenacious*; he wasn't giving up until he had satisfactory answers' – or retentive – 'He had a *tenacious* memory and you could never rely on his having forgotten, never mind forgiven.' Someone with a lingering illness might *hang on tenaciously to life,* while a superstition that most people had discarded might prove *tenacious* in remote country areas.

❦

tendentious

Connected with *tendency*, this means showing a tendency or bias, but usually in a disagreeable way: *a tendentious analysis of a sacred text*, for example, would be expected to promote controversy.

❦

tremulous

Trembling, showing fear, often used of a voice. '"Who's there?" she called *tremulously*. It was dark in the basement and she didn't want to go down on her own.' You might also open a letter *with tremulous hands* if you were afraid it contained bad news, or *put on a tremulous smile* if you were nervous about going into a room full of strangers.

❦

trepidation

Often in the expression *fear and trepidation*, this strictly means rather more than fear. It's often used loosely: in 'I asked with some *trepidation* if he had had his exam results, because I knew he had found the course difficult', it means little more than nervousness, but genuine trepidation makes you shake with fright or anxiety. A recently qualified teacher might feel *trepidation* about taking her first class, or an actor about playing King Lear, given that so many great actors had done it before. The adjective *trepid* is rarely used, but its opposite *intrepid* describes someone who feels no trepidation and happily goes into unexplored territory. The noun for this boldness is *intrepidity* or *intrepidness*; *intrepidation* doesn't exist.

ubiquitous

Seemingly everywhere at once, turning up everywhere: *a ubiquitous television presenter* appears to be on every show you watch; *the ubiquitous coriander* will be on every 'fusion' menu, and *the ubiquitous box hedge* in every formal garden. There's an undercurrent of, 'Oh, no, not again' about it.

unanimous

Of one mind, all in agreement, often referring to voting: 'He was elected *unanimously*; no one expressed any doubts at all' or 'It was a *unanimous* decision to cancel the outing; we all agreed that it was too expensive.'

CHAPTER FOUR

Let's Give It Some Thought

English seems to have an extraordinary number of words to do with secrecy – is someone trying to confuse us? We're also rich in words for thinking things over, for how we perceive things, presenting the results of our pondering and the way other people react. And that's what this chapter is about.

abstruse

Unhelpfully, this is easiest to define by the use of other *abstruse* words such as ESOTERIC or *recondite*. All mean 'hard to understand'; *abstruse* comes from the Latin for 'thrust away' and *recondite* for 'hidden away', but that is a very subtle distinction. You could have an *abstruse* specialist subject (such as an obscure branch of mathematics); an *abstruse* point of logic or philosophy (understood only by those who have studied it in depth); and in either case the sources on which you drew to back up your argument would be *recondite*.

◦▰◦

anticipate

Purists would say this is a much misused word; pragmatists would argue that it is so *widely* misused that its 'inaccurate' sense has become acceptable. Let's look at both and you can choose. The 'pure' meaning comes in a sentence such as 'She *anticipated* the baby's arrival by buying a pram and a cot' – she did something in advance of something else. She could also take evasive action: 'She *anticipated* the accident by putting the precious vase out of reach [and as a result the accident didn't happen].' The purists are still happy. They become unhappy with 'She *anticipated* that he would arrive at eight o'clock, so planned to have supper later than usual.' In that last example, *anticipate* means nothing more than *expect* and the sort of dictionary that expresses an opinion will tell you that this use is 'avoided by careful writers and speakers of English'.

◦▰◦

arcane

This too means obscure, but is closer to ESOTERIC than either is to ABSTRUSE or recondite (see page 87): to understand something *arcane*, you need to be initiated into its secrets. The word carries a suggestion of black or white magic – the two main divisions in a pack of Tarot cards are called the Major and Minor *Arcana*.

cerebral

Pertaining to the brain, involving the intellect rather than the emotions. The study of Ancient Greek, for example, might be described as *a cerebral occupation* and might be undertaken by *a cerebral person* who, in his turn, might write *a cerebral commentary* on the works of Plato. Such a commentary would analyse what Plato had to say but wouldn't tell you how the commentator felt about it.

clandestine

Secret, usually for an immoral or illicit purpose. *Clandestine meetings* are unlikely to involve your spouse; if they are work-related there won't be anyone taking minutes, because there's something slightly subversive going on.

coherent

Sticking together logically, as in *a coherent narrative* – one that starts at the beginning, goes on till it comes to the end and then stops. The verb is *to cohere* and the noun *cohesion*, but both are used more often in science than in general conversation.

commensurate

The middle part of this word is to do with measuring
and *com-* means *with* or *together*, so something that
is *commensurate* with something else is measured
alongside it and found appropriate, fitting, in the correct
proportions. 'Salary *commensurate* with experience' is
often seen in job advertisements, while a prison sentence
should be *commensurate* with the seriousness of the crime.

concomitant

Existing together, accompanying, going metaphorically
hand in hand. In a memorable line from the great Ealing
comedy *Kind Hearts and Coronets*, Alec Guinness as
the Parson (one of his eight roles in the film) describes
a stained-glass window as having 'all the exuberance
of Chaucer without, happily, any of the *concomitant*
crudities of his period'. Anyone who has read Chaucer will
understand exactly what he means; anyone who hasn't can
have a fair guess.

confluence

A flowing together, as in the *confluence of two rivers*, but
also of people gathering together in one place. Figuratively,
the word can mean anything else that flows together, such
as *a confluence of ideas* or *a confluence of factors* leading to
success or failure.

consensus

A general agreement: 'Although we didn't take a vote, the *consensus* seemed to be in favour.' The frequently heard *general consensus* and *consensus of opinion* are both TAUTOLOGIES.

∾

continuum

Anything that has a continuous structure, with one part flowing smoothly into the next: the word is the neuter form of the Latin for *continuous*, which means unbroken, uninterrupted (as opposed to *continual*, happening over and over again). It's often heard in the expression *space-time continuum*, a concept in physics that fuses time (thought of as the fourth dimension) with the three dimensions of the everyday world. But it can also be applied in a wider context: as long ago as the 1950s the geographer A. E. Smailes was writing about *an urban–rural continuum* as opposed to a clear distinction between town and country.

∾

covert

From the Old French for 'covered' and closely related to the *coverts* in which pheasants and other game birds lurk, this means concealed or secret but is more likely to refer to an emotion or to an action than to a meeting. You might give someone *a covert glance* if you were involved in a CLANDESTINE relationship with them; you might even *covertly* hold their hand under the table. Spies may be engaged in *covert operations,* while an institution may practise *covert sexism* by finding an excuse not to promote members of whichever gender it is prejudiced against.

cryptic

Applied most commonly to those crosswords that, if you aren't in on the code, seem ABSTRUSE or even ARCANE. But it isn't just crossword clues that are *cryptic*: most fictional detectives are given to *cryptic utterances* before they are ready to reveal all, while *a cryptic remark* may simply be one that you don't understand. The word comes from the Greek for 'a secret place' – hence the English *crypt*, the underground chamber beneath a church; anything *cryptic* is secret, mysterious, difficult to make sense of. The use of the word 'code' at the start of this entry is no accident: *cryptography* means writing in codes, *cryptanalysis* is breaking them, while many other words beginning in *crypto-* refer to codes and secrecy. *A crypto-communist,* for example, is one who is secretive about his allegiance or beliefs.

delineate

To draw a clear outline of (both literally and figuratively) or to portray something clearly in words. The American 'founding father' Thomas Jefferson put it like this: 'Do you want to know who you are? Don't ask. Act! Action will *delineate* and define you', and Jane Austen referred in *Northanger Abbey* to a novel's ability to provide 'the happiest *delineation*' of the varieties of human nature, meaning to create a great cast of characters.

demur

To raise an objection, to show reluctance. It's an intransitive verb, which means you don't *demur something*, you just *demur*: 'It was suggested we put it to the vote but the president *demurred*.' The act of demurring is a *demurral*.

dilemma

The fact that this word is frequently preceded by 'on the horns of' gives a clue to its correct use: it is a choice between two equally unpleasant alternatives. There are two key points here: the choice is between two and only two things, and they are both bad. Deciding where to go on holiday is not a dilemma unless only two places are available to you and it is cyclone season in both. See also QUANDARY.

discombobulated

A jokey word meaning exactly what it sounds as if it means: confused, disconcerted, 'thrown' in a big way. You might be *discombobulated* by an interruption or by the appearance of an unexpected guest; on a bad day you could be generally *discombobulated*, not with it and unable to cope with the many questions that life throws at you.

discrete

Separate, individual, consisting of distinct parts. A reference book might have *discrete* sections on literature and science, while the right software allows *discrete* programs to communicate with one another. Of a similar derivation but entirely different in meaning is *discreet*, which means tactful, able to keep a secret, unobtrusive. You might cough *discreetly* to attract someone's attention, employ a *discreet* person as your private secretary or wear a *discreet* amount of make-up if you didn't want to look flashy.

disparate

The middle part of this word is *par* meaning 'equal', so two things that are *disparate* (or show *disparity*) are unequal, essentially different. A man who married a woman thirty years his junior (or indeed his senior) might expect comments on the *disparity of their ages*; an art gallery showing paintings from various countries and centuries might try to weave together *disparate styles*.

◦◦◦

dissemble

The *semble* part comes from the same root as *semblance*, *resembling* and other words connected with appearances. The prefix *dis-* gives a negative meaning, so the two together mean to disguise one's feelings, motives or actions and generally to behave in a hypocritical fashion. The largely forgotten eighteenth-century poet Isaac Bickerstaffe produced this lovely couplet under the title 'An Expostulation':

> Perhaps it was right to *dissemble* your love,
> But—why did you kick me downstairs?

Here the lady was presumably dissembling out of modesty, but when the Book of Common Prayer gives in its version of Psalm 12, 'They do but flatter with their lips, and dissemble in their double hearts', we need be in no doubt of the disapproving tone. To *dissimulate* means almost exactly the same thing and is related to words for likeness such as *simulate, similarity* and *flight simulator*.

◦◦◦

eclectic

Selecting from a wide range of sources. The gallery
mentioned under DISPARATE (page 93) would have *an
eclectic collection*; a person who enjoyed Mozart, Al Jolson
and Lady Gaga could claim to have *an eclectic taste in
music*.

elucidate

As Sherlock Holmes said in *The Hound of the Baskervilles*,
when referring to the importance of an old boot as a
clue: 'The more *outré* and GROTESQUE an incident is the
more carefully it deserves to be examined, and the very
point which appears to complicate a case is, when duly
considered and scientifically handled, the one which is
most likely to *elucidate* it.' The key part of the word is *lucid*,
which means clear and easy to understand. *To elucidate* is
to make clear something that has previously been unclear,
to draw meaning out of it, as only Sherlock Holmes could.

embroil

From the French for to mingle or confuse, this means
to involve (usually yourself) in a conflict or a state of
confusion: 'I don't know how I came to *embroil* myself
in that argument; I might have known I couldn't win.'
Although the noun *embroilment* does exist, it surely has
less charm than the form we have borrowed from the
Italian: *imbroglio*. Don't pronounce the *g*, roll the rest of the
word round your tongue and see how much pleasure
it gives.

entail

To impose, to bring about as a necessary result, to require: 'Yes, we can meet the deadline, but it will *entail* a lot of overtime.' Or 'I can't commit to joining the choir until I know exactly how much rehearsal time it will *entail*.'

❧

equivocal

Literally 'calling equally', this means 'ambiguous, of doubtful or double meaning'. *An equivocal statement* is not necessarily a lie but it is probably guilty of OBFUSCATION, of deliberately concealing the truth; *equivocal evidence* would not convince anyone beyond reasonable doubt. Related to this is the verb *to equivocate*, to use equivocal statements to conceal the truth, much the same as to PREVARICATE.

❧

esoteric

Another word with a precise and a looser meaning. From the Greek for inner or within, the original meaning is 'understandable only to the initiated, those with special knowledge': *an esoteric ritual*, perhaps. More generally, the word can be used to mean hard to understand, obscure: *an esoteric knowledge of postage stamps* or *the esoteric aims of a fringe religious group*.

❧

farrago

From the Latin for cattle feed, this means a mishmash, a hotchpotch, a confused mixture. You often hear *a farrago of nonsense* or *a farrago of lies*, although the nineteenth-century Prime Minister and poet George Canning also referred to *this farrago of cowardice, cunning and cant* (an expression, I venture to suggest, that you have to pronounce very carefully indeed).

feign

Pronounced 'fain', this means to pretend, to put on a show of, as in 'She *feigned* indifference, but deep down she was very upset.' It's included here in part because there are so many words to confuse it with. *Fain*, for example, is an old-fashioned word for willingly, as in 'I would *fain* come with you, but the journey would be too much for me.' *Feint* (pronounced 'faint') is related to *feign* when it means a mock attack in fencing, and related to *faint* when it refers to the light, thin lines printed on ruled paper.

fortuitous

Strictly speaking, *fortuitous* does not mean *fortunate*. It means happening by chance, accidental. However, the looser use is now so widespread that most people would assume that *a fortuitous encounter* was more than just a chance meeting: it was a lucky or happy chance.

gallimaufry

Another jumble or hotchpotch (see FARRAGO, page 95), this time from a French word for a stew. One of the earliest people to use it in the figurative sense was the Elizabethan poet Edmund Spenser; in 1579 he complained that 'some' (he doesn't specify who) had decided that English was too barren a language for literary writing, so had borrowed words from Italian, French *et al* and 'have made our English tongue a *gallimaufray* or hodgepodge of all other speeches'. This was long before the outposts of the British

Empire had brought us words such as veranda, tattoo and ketchup and made the language the real *gallimaufry* it is today – goodness knows what Spenser would have thought if he'd still been with us.

☙

gambit

An opening move – originally in chess, now in almost anything. Asking 'How do you know our host?' is *a conversational gambit*, for example, while suggesting a one per cent pay rise may be *a negotiating gambit*, with everyone knowing that it is merely an initial offer. *An opening gambit,* although commonly used, is a TAUTOLOGY.

☙

gnomic

A *gnome* – when it is not the kind that lives in the garden or runs banks in Zurich – is an aphorism, a short, PITHY saying. *Gnomic* is the adjective derived from it and it is applied to sayings that contain a general truth but are perhaps rather pompous. Dr Josephine Guy of the University of Nottingham, reviewing *The Oxford English Literary History: The Victorians – Volume 8* by Philip Davis, came up with this wonderful example:

> The General Editor's preface claims that '[l]iterary history is distinct from political history, but a historical understanding of literature cannot be divorced from cultural and intellectual revolutions or the effects of social change' ... This (perhaps deliberately) *gnomic* statement obscures the vexed question of the epistemological role of literary works *qua* literary works.

I share this with you without further comment.

grandiose

Well, grand, obviously, but pretentiously grand, imposing and rather forbidding. Sigmund Freud is quoted as saying that 'America is the most *grandiose* experiment the world has seen, but, I am afraid, it is not going to be a success' – a strange observation, given that he visited the US some 133 years after the Declaration of Independence, when Henry Ford was doing great things with the Model T and the young country was generally doing okay. On a smaller scale, you can make *grandiose gestures*, have *grandiose visions* or compose *a grandiose orchestral work*, but they will all be a bit over the top.

gravitas

The Latin for heaviness or seriousness, this is now often used in the sense of how seriously something is perceived by the wider world – 'Having three PhDs on board lends *gravitas* to our research' or 'He may be brilliant at soundbites, but he lacks *gravitas*.' There is an exact Latin opposite: the late MP Julian Critchley recorded that, when he was a *frivolous* young man, a rather grave colleague accused him of *levitas*. Sadly, that superb scholarly put-down hasn't made it into English dictionaries; you have to stick to *levity* or *frivolity*, both of which imply misplaced light-heartedness: *a frivolous remark* (trying to be funny in a serious situation), *a suggestion of levity in his* DEMEANOUR (pulling faces during a meeting, perhaps).

hubris

Pride comes before a fall, they say, and the Ancient Greeks had a word for that particular sort of misplaced pride: *hubris*. They used it with reference to their classical tragedies to describe the flaw in the hero's character – excessive ambition or arrogance, for example – that led to his downfall (see NEMESIS). An exhibition at the National Portrait Gallery in London on the theme of the First World War emphasized that this failing wasn't confined to classical Greece: its commentary on state portraits of leaders of the period remarked that these paintings 'evoked those values and attitudes that, in part, were ingredients in creating the conditions for war ... [They] transmit pride and grandeur, but also hubris.' Considering the huge social upheavals that war brought, this has to be described as a 'fair comment'.

hypothetical

A *hypothesis* is a bit like a theory – an idea that has been put forward, looks probable, might even be true, but is as yet unproven. *To use something as a working hypothesis* is to go forward on this basis, to assume that it is right and see what happens. *Hypothetical* is the adjective derived from this and is frequently used in the phrase *a hypothetical question*, one that supposes something is true when it may or may not be: '*Hypothetically*, where would you like to go on holiday if we could afford it?'

incognito

The only way to travel if you are famous and want to avoid attention. This is the Italian for unknown, and it is used in English to mean 'keeping your identity secret' – 'He went to Mexico *incognito* so that he could holiday in peace.' If you were being precise, a woman would travel *incognita*. The word can also be a noun, denoting (infrequently) either the person who is *incognito* or the form of their disguise: 'Despite my huge dark glasses he saw through my *incognito*.'

infinitesimal

Tiny, tiny, tiny, immeasurably small. 'I have an *infinitesimal* amount of sugar in my coffee because I can't bear to give it up altogether.'

inscrutable

The key here is the *scrut* part, which comes from the Latin for to examine and appears also in *scrutiny* and *scrutinize*. *Inscrutable* therefore means impossible to understand, analyse or interpret. You could put *an inscrutable expression* on your face so that people didn't know what you were thinking, or make *an inscrutable remark* so that they didn't know what you were talking about.

intromission

The act of putting something inside something else; an insertion. In Jonathan Swift's *Gulliver's Travels* the hero speaks disapprovingly of people who take purges and emetics, for, he says, nature intended the mouth 'only for the *intromission* of solids and liquids'. The word is also used in a sexual sense that we needn't go into here. It is not to be confused with an *intermission*, which is the interval between two parts of a film or play. The rule here: *inter* means between, while *intro* and *intra* (as in the *intranet*, which enables workers to communicate with people within their own company) mean inside, within.

irrefutable

That cannot be *refuted*, disproved or denied. Usually *irrefutable evidence,* evidence that will prove someone's guilt or innocence beyond doubt, or *an irrefutable argument*, one to which there is no answer.

labyrinthine

A *labyrinth* is a maze (the original was in Knossos in Crete, where the monster known as the Minotaur was confined); thus *labyrinthine* means maze-like, complicated and confusing. It can be literal – perhaps referring to the alleys in a medieval town – or figurative, applied to arguments, trains of thought or long, complex sentences. See also BYZANTINE.

licit

Legal, above board – less commonly used than its opposite, *illicit*, and frequently applied to the lawful side of something that is often unlawful: *licit arms dealing,* for example, or *the licit use of class A drugs.*

Lilliputian

Another word for very small, this time from the island country of *Lilliput*, created by Jonathan Swift in *Gulliver's Travels*, where the people were no more than 15cm tall. *Lilliputian* can refer to anything small, not just people: *a Lilliputian chihuahua* would fit in a celebrity's handbag or *a Lilliputian computer* sit snugly in a back pocket.

maelstrom

This is from the Dutch for whirlpool and in English is used in a figurative sense for any state of violent confusion: you can have *a political maelstrom*, *a maelstrom of* (particularly confusing) *events* or *a maelstrom of* (particularly congested) *traffic*.

minuscule

Note the spelling: that middle vowel isn't an *i*. A *minuscule* letter is strictly speaking a lower-case one, to use the old-fashioned printing term; a small one, not a capital (which is upper case or *majuscule*). However, *minuscule* is widely used to describe anything small – you could write *minuscule letters* in *minuscule handwriting* or chop a piece of meat into *minuscule pieces* to feed it to a puppy. *Majuscule*, oddly enough, has not broadened in meaning and isn't generally used with reference to anything other than printing.

minutiae

Details, particularly tiny, fastidious ones: 'I'm a broad-brushstroke person; I let my assistant deal with the *minutiae*.'

nonplus

From the Latin for 'no more', in the sense of 'there is nothing more to be said or done', this means to perplex utterly, to confound: 'He was *nonplussed* by the news – he hadn't expected that at all' or 'I am *nonplussed* by the data I'm supposed to analyse – I don't know where to start.'

obfuscation

Derived from the Latin for dark, this is another word meaning perplexity or bewilderment (see previous entry and various others in this chapter). This time there is a sense of deliberateness about it: if you are *obfuscating* you are intentionally pulling the wool over someone's eyes, perhaps by using medical or legal jargon that is unintelligible to an outsider. The ironic advice that good writing should 'avoid unnecessary prolixity and eschew *obfuscation*' has become a cliché, but is – like many clichés – founded in truth.

oblivious

Although this derives from a word for forgetfulness (and is connected to *oblivion*, 'the condition of being forgotten'), *oblivious* means not so much forgetful as unaware: 'She blundered on, *oblivious* to the fact that she was offending everyone within earshot.'

ostensible

The first part of this word means to show and also gives us
OSTENTATIOUS. *Ostensible* means apparent but unlikely to
be true: 'His *ostensible* reason for the visit was to see his
elderly aunt, but he also looked over her possessions and
wondered what he might expect to inherit.'

paramount

Of the greatest importance, often in the expression *of
paramount importance*: 'It is of *paramount* importance that
the evidence be ready by the first day of the trial.' Airlines
often tell you that your safety is *paramount*; in divorce
hearings a court might consider the wellbeing of the
children *paramount*. The *mount* part of this word is related
to *mountain*, so it really is scaling the heights.

perspicacious

Perceptive, observant. Not so much in the literal, using-
your-eyes sense as in the emotional/intellectual, insightful
one: *a perspicacious remark* cuts right to the heart of the
issue.

peruse

This is a posh word for 'read', but it means reading with
care and/or in an unhurried fashion. You might, for
example, take the newspaper to the café on a Saturday
morning to *peruse* the sports pages at your leisure.

precedent

A term from legal speak now used in a broader context. In law, a *precedent* is a decision or an interpretation of the law, made in an earlier case, on which a judge may draw when ruling in the current case. In the wider world, it can mean more or less any earlier event that justifies a current one: 'There is no *precedent* for taking time off to attend a niece's wedding.' Be warned, away from the law courts, precedents are often undesirable, as in: 'It would set a dangerous *precedent* to employ someone with no experience just because he is charming and handsome.'

precipitate

As an adjective, with the last syllable swallowed so that it comes out rather like 'tit', this means much the same as IMPETUOUS: hasty and ill-considered. *A precipitate action* is likely to get you into trouble because you have rushed in, giving no thought to the consequences. *A precipitate action* may also *precipitate* a crisis – this time with the last syllable given its full value, to rhyme with *eight,* and meaning to cause to happen prematurely.

predicament

A difficult situation, but not as difficult as a DILEMMA – with luck, patience or common sense you should find your way out of a predicament. Unless, that is, you are talking about *the human predicament*, the philosophical concept of humans being aware of their own inevitable death and therefore of the meaninglessness of life. There's no easy way out of that.

presage

Pronounced either *pree-sage* or *pressage*, as a verb this means to give early warning of, to foreshadow. A red sky at night traditionally *presages* a fine day.

prevaricate

This is a verb meaning not exactly to lie but certainly to be economical with the truth: to mislead or avoid answering the question. "'You said those flowers weren't from you,' she accused. "No," he replied, "you asked me directly and I *prevaricated*." You sometimes hear *prevaricate* used as if it meant PROCRASTINATE (see next entry), but there is a clear difference: the procrastinator merely delays while the prevaricator intends to deceive.

procrastinate

Cras is Latin for tomorrow, so procrastinating in the strictest sense means putting off until tomorrow. But it is generally used to mean putting off for an indefinite period, probably as long as you can get away with it.

providential

Happening through the workings of Providence, because 'somebody up there' is looking out for you. Hence, fortunate, with or without the intervention of the Almighty. There is also the implication of good timing: *a providential inheritance* would not only provide you with money but would enable you to pay off your debts before the bank foreclosed.

putative

From the Latin for to think, this means supposed, reputed, but, as with OSTENSIBLE, there's the implication that whatever is suggested isn't true or proven. *A putative romance* between two Hollywood stars might have been cooked up by the studio's publicity department, while *a putative diabetes treatment* is one that hasn't yet been tested and about which the person using the expression has doubts.

quandary

A difficult situation, one in which you don't know what to do: 'I'm in a *quandary*. Mother will be offended if I don't wear the necklace she gave me, but it really doesn't go with my dress' or 'The school had to deal with the *quandary*: should they let disruptive pupils stay and disturb the whole class, or send them home, where there may be no one to keep an eye on them?' A quandary differs from a DILEMMA in that it may offer you more than two possibilities, but that makes it all the more fraught.

ratiocination

A posh word for working something out logically or methodically. Alessandro Volta, the Italian physicist after whom the volt is named, is quoted as saying, 'The language of experiment is more authoritative than any reasoning: facts can destroy our *ratiocination* – not vice versa.' This isn't a word many people use, unless they are Italian physicists or high-powered philosophers, but it does no harm to know what it means – you never know whom you're going to fall into conversation with on the bus.

recherché

A French word meaning 'thoroughly searched for', this is yet another in the ABSTRUSE/ESOTERIC/recondite category. You probably wouldn't understand a *recherché* expression or concept unless you belonged to some 'in crowd' or other, and the person using such an expression might be deliberately trying to keep you out of that inner circle: 'He tried to explain how Jung differed from Freud, but the words he used were too *recherché* for me.'

repository

A resting place, a place where something precious may safely be left: 'The bank vault was the only safe *repository* for the family jewels.' A *repository* may also be a trustworthy person: 'She was the only *repository* for my confession, because I knew she wouldn't gossip about it.'

rudimentary

Basic, not fully developed: 'I have a *rudimentary* understanding of chess – I know that the bishop goes diagonally and the knight leaps about – but I don't play well.' You could, in the same context, say, 'I understand the *rudiments* of chess.'

ruminate

The *rumen* is the first compartment (of four) in the stomach of a cow, deer or other cud-chewing animal; such animals are zoologically described as *ruminants* and what they are doing when chewing the cud is *ruminating*. When those of us whose stomachs don't have four compartments ruminate, we are thinking slowly and ponderously. It doesn't mean that we are stupid, but it does mean that we are going to take our time coming to a conclusion.

☙

seminal

From the Latin for seed and therefore connected with *semen*, this can mean either basic, undeveloped (*a seminal idea*, one that hasn't been thought through yet) or fundamental, very influential and important – *the seminal text on philology* would be the one you absolutely had to read, assuming you were studying philology.

☙

sentient

From the Latin for feel (and therefore connected with *sentiment* and SENSIBILITY), this means being able to perceive or feel things by the senses (sight, touch etc.), being able to receive sensations. *A sentient being* is one who is conscious of the world around; and *sentient powers* are sometimes differentiated from *intellectual* ones, which involve thought.

☙

sibylline

In Roman mythology the Sibyl was an enormously old woman (or one of several) reputed to have the power of prophecy; much of her/their wisdom was contained within the Sibylline Books, kept under careful guard by Roman patricians and consulted at times of crisis in the Republic and Empire. Sadly, most of the Sibyl's pronouncements were obscure and difficult to interpret. Thus *sibylline* has come to mean not only prophetic but mysterious with it: 'In her later years, my mother was given to *sibylline remarks* that sounded profound but left us all wondering what she was talking about.'

☙❧

solecism

This has specialist meanings in the world of grammar, but in a social context it means a mistake, a gaffe or a violation of etiquette. It would once, for example, have been considered a solecism to say 'serviette' rather than 'napkin' or 'mirror' rather than 'looking glass'; nowadays you are more likely to be censured for making a tactless reference to someone's ex or expressing strong political views which offend a fellow guest at a dinner party.

☙❧

sophistry

A deliberately misleading form of argument, plausible but unsound. The eighteenth-century poet Alexander Pope linked it to other forms of deception: 'The Parson's Cant, the Lawyer's Sophistry, Lord's Quibble, Critick's Jest'. They all, he says fatalistically, end in silence and death. See also MERETRICIOUS and SPECIOUS.

Sophistry derives from the same Greek root as *sophisticated*; the original meaning of this was to make someone less natural by educating them. This came to be seen as much the same as corrupting them and *sophisticated tastes* were considered pretentious. The modern, more complimentary sense of well-educated and cultured dates only from the late nineteenth century.

☙❧

stultify

To stultify is literally to render stupid, but more generally to make something or someone useless or ineffective: *a stultifying routine* at work would make you too bored to achieve anything, while *stultifying heat* would mean it was too hot to move or even to think.

❦

subliminal

Literally 'under the threshold', this describes information that you absorb without being aware of it. *Subliminal advertising*, now illegal in many countries, might flash a product's name on to the cinema screen so briefly that the viewer was not consciously aware of it, but the brain had nevertheless registered it.

❦

surreptitious

Another near-synonym for CLANDESTINE or COVERT, this describes something done by stealth. If you came quietly into the room you might simply not want to disturb anyone; if you entered *surreptitiously*, it would be with the intention of eavesdropping or of removing some damning piece of evidence.

❦

synthesis

If *analysis* is taking things apart and studying how their separate components contribute to the whole, then *synthesis* is putting them back together again and forming something that is greater than the sum of the parts. According to the American R. Buckminster Fuller, a designer is 'an emerging *synthesis* of artist, inventor, mechanic, objective economist and evolutionary strategist'. Considering that Mr Fuller was described as an architect, systems theorist, author, designer, inventor and futurist, he should have known.

꩜

vicarious

Experienced through the feelings or actions of another: 'We get *vicarious* pleasure from our daughter's working with famous people, even though we rarely meet them ourselves' or 'The regional courts held *vicarious* powers because the king could not preside over all of them.' *Vicarious* comes from the same source as *vicar*, originally a clergyman who substituted for another, and as *vice presidents, vice admirals* and *vice chairs*, who are all one step down from the top rank and able to take over if necessary.

꩜

voluminous

Of great size or extent, prolific. A large woman could be dressed in *a voluminous caftan*; enthusiastic letter-writers could produce *a voluminous correspondence.* This sort of volume has nothing to do with noise: *voluminous evidence* in a court case would fill a number of *volumes*, but it wouldn't necessarily be spoken loudly.

CHAPTER FIVE

The Rough with the Smooth

This chapter contains a selection of words about making things easier or harder for ourselves and some of the feelings this may provoke. It's also about the way we rub along together, money, the lack of it and the things it can buy.

alienate

To make someone feel unfriendly towards you: 'During his time in office he has managed to *alienate* the entire electorate; he hasn't a hope of getting in again.' In addition to alienating a person, you may – if you are careless – *alienate their affections,* making them dislike you or at least cease to be on your side.

alleviate

To lighten, as in a burden: you might *alleviate someone's responsibilities* by doing some of their work for them, or *alleviate their sorrow* by being kind and sympathetic. The word is related to *levity*, which is discussed under GRAVITAS.

ameliorate

To make or become better: 'If a parent can't make himself rich, he at least wants to *ameliorate* his children's prospects' or 'They were at each other's throats last time I saw them, but I gather that the situation has *ameliorated* somewhat.'

annihilate

Nihil is the Latin for nothing, so this is to reduce to nothing, to destroy utterly. A plague of locusts might literally *annihilate the crops*; figuratively speaking, an intimidating acquaintance might *annihilate you* – effectively reduce you to nothing through embarrassment or humiliation – with a withering look or a biting remark. Although the original meaning is every bit as precise as that of DECIMATE, page 118, the loose figurative use doesn't seem to spark anything like as much debate.

❧

assuage

A verb meaning to relieve or soothe, as in *to assuage someone's feelings* (make them feel better) or *to assuage their thirst* (give them a glass of water). It's loosely connected with *suave*; both come from the Latin for 'sweet, pleasant' and this is a sweet, pleasant word.

❧

badinage

Light-hearted, witty chat or banter: 'The *badinage* between the two presenters must have been scripted, but it sounded very natural.'

❧

calamity

A very great disaster, often a natural disaster or a period of political or social upheaval rather than a personal crisis. In Shakespeare's *Romeo and Juliet*, however, Friar Lawrence personifies the misfortune when he tells Romeo:

Affliction is enamour'd of thy parts
And thou are wedded to *calamity*.

He's going on to say that Romeo is to be banished, so this is serious stuff.

❧

catalyst

In chemistry, a *catalyst* is something whose presence causes or speeds up a reaction, but which doesn't itself change. In the rest of life, it is merely something that causes a change: an injection of money could be described as a *catalyst* for the regeneration of a community, while the arrival of a sociable new employee could be the *catalyst* for more office parties.

catharsis

This has specific meanings in both philosophy and psychoanalysis, but in everyday speech it means 'emotional relief, especially of repressed emotion', so writing an autobiographical novel could be one way of achieving *catharsis*. The expression is also used of dealing with mourning: 'The candlelit vigil brought a degree of *catharsis* to the grieving relatives.' The adjective is *cathartic*, as in *a cathartic experience.*

chagrin

This is a French word, so pronounce the initial sound as *sh* and the last syllable more like *ran* than *rin*. It means a combination of annoyance, hurt and discomfort: 'Much to my *chagrin*, I heard the news through the grapevine – it would have been kinder to tell me yourself.'

chronic

Related to the Greek for time (and other English words such as *chronology* and *chronicle*, both of which list events in the order in which they occurred), this means long-lasting, constantly recurring or habitual: *a chronic illness* is one that develops slowly and lasts a long time, as opposed to *an acute condition* which flares up rapidly and then, with any luck, goes away again. *A chronic gambler* would have a lifelong habit. The popular use of the word to mean 'dreadful', as in 'He's a *chronic* public speaker; you'll be bored to tears' is, as the dictionaries say, 'avoided by careful users of English'.

⚬≋⚬

compunction

'I had no *compunction* in doing that' means 'I did it without a qualm, without hesitation or regret.' This is another word from the Latin for a point or prick (see PUNCTILIOUS), so something that does make you feel compunction causes a twinge of guilt.

⚬≋⚬

confabulate

To chat, to converse, as in the common abbreviation *confab*, a putting-our-heads-together-in-order-to-decide. The often-heard *conflab,* appealing though it is, is wrong.

⚬≋⚬

cornucopia

Literally 'horn of plenty', a *cornucopia* has been a symbol of abundance since ancient times, traditionally depicted as a goat's horn overflowing with corn, fruit and flowers. From that specific application the word has come to mean abundance of any kind. You can have a *cornucopia of dishes* on a buffet table, a *cornucopia of information* if you have access to a number of useful websites, or *a cornucopia of acting talent* in an all-star movie.

⚬≋⚬

crucial

From the Latin for a cross and related to *crux*, as in *the crux of the matter*, the vital or decisive point, this means supremely important, involving a critical, often final decision. 'It is *crucial* that he attends the meeting' might, in casual use, simply mean that it was very important; strictly speaking it means that the meeting will fall apart or not take place if he doesn't turn up. Similarly, 'Research into animal behaviour plays a *crucial* role in our conservation efforts' means that the efforts are meaningless without the research.

cumulative

Building up, growing in quantity step by step: often in the expression *the cumulative effect*: 'The *cumulative* effect of all those lessons is that she is now a confident and skilled driver.'

debacle

This is a French word and shouldn't be pronounced *debackle;* it's more like *day-bahk–ull.* It means a sudden collapse or defeat or, less formally, a fiasco. In a political context, something like *the pensions debacle* or *the funding debacle* means that there was a lot of fuss about the issue, the government came out of it badly and nothing much was resolved.

decimate

This is a word that will keep the purists chained to the barricades until the Day of Judgement. In Roman times, it meant to kill one in ten – it was a punishment designed to make a culprit own up so that his comrades didn't die unnecessarily. Today, many people use it as a synonym for *devastate*, to destroy, lay waste or, if you are being mathematical about it, to kill perhaps nine out of ten. Some dictionaries describe this use as 'loose'; at least one gives 'to destroy or kill a large proportion of' as its first meaning. I'm going to stick my neck out and say that in modern life we don't have much use for a word meaning precisely 'to kill one in ten' and that, unless we are talking about Ancient Rome, this is a distinction hardly worth preserving. But I shall expect angry letters from the purists.

desuetude

Disuse, not being used or practised any more; a word that perhaps has a tinge of regret to it: 'The habit of dressing for dinner has fallen into *desuetude*' suggests that you would love the opportunity to show off the tiara. It's a rather formal, literary word that isn't used a great deal, but surely deserves to be rescued from its near-desuetude.

discomfiture

Embarrassment, discomfort or the frustration of one's plans. 'He couldn't hide his *discomfiture* when his mother turned up unexpectedly'; or, to use the related verb, 'The Union army was utterly *discomfited* by Lee's superior generalship.'

dissipate

To dissipate is to spread around in a wasteful way: 'They *dissipated* their resources so thoroughly that they had no money left to pay the wages.' The act of doing this is called *dissipation*, which also means unrestrained self-indulgence: 'the *dissipation* of dancing until two in the morning'.

❧

dissonance

Literally, a discordant combination of sounds; figuratively, anything else that doesn't 'ring true' or is 'out of tune'. *To sound a dissonant note* may be to make a mistake on the piano or to make a disparaging comment when everyone else is full of praise.

❧

dystopia

When, in 1516, Thomas More wrote about his perfect but impracticable society, he named the island where it existed Utopia, from the Greek for 'no place'. The word caught on and people who believed in such a place were called *utopians*. Somewhere along the line, however, More's Greek *ou-*, meaning 'no', became confused with *eu-*, meaning 'pleasant, good' (see EUPHEMISM). So when the Victorian philosopher John Stuart Mill wanted a word for people who believed in something too *bad* to be practicable, he used the opposite of *eu-*, *dys-*, meaning abnormal, faulty or bad, and came up with *dys-topians*. It may have made the scholars shudder, but a *dystopia* soon became a place, often a society of the future, where everything is awful; *dystopian novels* were a feature of twentieth-century literature, with a long list headed by George Orwell's *1984*.

❧

effectuate

To bring something into effect, to make it happen: *to effectuate a change of government* might be a EUPHEMISM for staging a coup. Changes are the things that are most often effectuated, but you could also *effectuate a new way of thinking* or *effectuate an improvement in living standards* – as long as the concept of change was in there somewhere.

enervate

This had some unpleasant early meanings, including to emasculate and to 'hamstring' a horse by cutting its tendons; nowadays it means merely to deprive of energy or vigour, to weaken either physically or morally. *An enervating climate* is so extreme that you can't bestir yourself to do anything, but you could also speak of *the enervating effects of wealth*, which mean you don't have to bestir yourself to do anything. What enervate doesn't mean is to get on someone's nerves.

enunciate

To pronounce words clearly and distinctly, or to express a proposition in clear, distinct terms. 'She *enunciated* the words of the song perfectly, so we didn't miss a syllable' or 'The new mayor's speech *enunciated* the principles that would guide him during his year in office.'

equilibrium

The first part of this word connects it to *equal* and *equilateral triangles*; the second means 'balance' or 'scales', as in the zodiac sign Libra. *Equilibrium* therefore means a state of balance. This can apply in a physical sense (as when two people sit opposite each other in a small boat so that it doesn't tip to one side or the other) or in a political one (as in 'European *equilibrium* was destroyed from the moment Napoleon seized control of France'). It can also have an emotional aspect: *to upset someone's equilibrium* is to throw someone – probably a placid, even-tempered person – metaphorically off balance.

❦

eschew

Nothing to do with chewing, this is instead connected with shy in the sense of 'to shy away from'. It means to avoid, to abstain from: you might *eschew chocolate for Lent* if you were feeling both abstemious and literary. In its translation of the Psalms, the Book of Common Prayer advises us to 'eschew evil and do good'; the King James version has the more prosaic 'depart from evil', but it obviously means the same thing.

❦

evoke

To summon up a feeling, especially a memory: 'Every time I smell lavender, it *evokes* that wonderful holiday in Provence.' Or to produce a result, to draw forth a response: 'When I said his beard needed trimming I wasn't expecting to *evoke* such a harsh reaction.' The adjective is *evocative*, as in 'The movie *L.A. Confidential* was made in the 1990s but it's *evocative* of the best of forties *film noir*.'

❦

exigency

A demand that cannot be avoided, often used in the plural: 'The *exigencies* of an actor's life are such that only the most successful make money and then they are too busy to spend it' or 'The *exigencies* of war demand sacrifices from us all.' The related adjective *exigent* means urgent – 'an *exigent* need to go home and have a bath' – or, of a person, demanding – 'I've never had such an *exigent* supervisor: she pulls me up on the slightest thing and often makes me rewrite whole essays.'

exiguous

Scanty or meagre; when applied to an income or a budget, barely enough to get by on. *Exiguity* needn't always refer to money; weak and unhealthy plant growth might produce *an exiguous covering of leaves*.

expatiate

To speak or write at length or in detail: 'There was no stopping Uncle John once he started to *expatiate* on his war experiences' or 'In his thesis, he *expatiated* on the advantages of an old-fashioned liberal education.' Not to be confused with *expatriate*, which means someone living outside their native country.

expedient

Generally convenient: that useful volume the 1549 Book of Common Prayer suggested it was *expedient* that baptisms be conducted in English, and it meant 'right and proper, suitable'. More recently the word has taken on a less attractive tone and has come to mean advantageous but not necessarily sticking to the moral high ground: *an expedient solution* to a problem might simply be to pay someone off. The related noun is *expediency*.

No such disparaging NUANCE attaches to the verb *to expedite*. It means to get something (probably a matter of business) done efficiently and quickly and the idea of '*expediting* the matter by introducing you to our production manager' is perfectly above board.

❦

expurgated
Related to *purge* and therefore with a suggestion of purifying, this describes something that has had the offensive bits cut out: *the expurgated version* of a film would have the sex and violence removed to make it suitable for family viewing.

❦

extirpate
To pull out by the roots; to eradicate completely: 'The church set out to *extirpate* heresy and blasphemy' or 'The colonists *extirpated* the indigenous people – after fifty years not one of them survived.'

❦

fracas
A French word, so the *s* is silent. This means an uproar, but – unlike a FURORE – always a quarrelsome and possibly a violent one. The *furore* on the night of the premiere would turn into a *fracas* if fans started hitting one another.

❦

frugal

This is one of those words that you probably wouldn't use to describe your own habits: there'd be a progression along the lines of 'I'm thrifty, you're frugal, he's mean.' But that's what *frugal* implies – avoiding waste and being perhaps just a little too careful with money. A meal may also be frugal, but you'd be advised not to say so if you've just been taken out to dinner.

❧

furore

British English has traditionally pronounced this word as three syllables; Americans spell it without the *e* and pronounce it as two. That pronunciation, if not yet the spelling, is drifting slowly but surely across the Atlantic. It means an uproar, often, but not always, an outraged one: 'Remember all the *furore* when house prices went up?' or, more positively, 'There was a great *furore* on the night of the premiere – thousands of people turned up to see Angelina Jolie.'

❧

gratification

This is the feeling of being *gratified*, a varying combination of pleased, grateful and flattered. 'I was gratified to be invited' is more than 'I was pleased to be invited', it means 'I was pleased because I felt I'd earned it and it was good to have my merits recognized.' As a verb, *to gratify* can also mean to satisfy a desire: 'He *gratified* his love of danger by signing up for skydiving lessons.'

❧

immolate

To sacrifice something of great value. *Self-immolation* is the hideous act of setting yourself on fire, but could also be something as trivial as giving up a fine Saturday afternoon to visit an ailing relative. You might also *immolate the rights of the individual* by sacrificing them to the good of society.

impecunious

A fancy alternative to 'having no money'. It may be that you are a spendthrift and that money just slips through your fingers; more probably you simply don't have it to spend.

inchoate

Pronounced *in-ko-ate*, this comes from the Latin for to yoke (as in attaching a team of oxen to a plough) and is most commonly an adjective, meaning 'just beginning or about to begin, undeveloped'. A religious or political movement that was in its infancy might have *inchoate* ideas, policies or organization; young children who hadn't yet learned or experienced a great deal, but of whom you had hope, could be described as having *inchoate intellects*. You might also say that 'Her quick apology stifled his *inchoate* rage' – in other words, he calmed down before he got around to exploding.

inure

Often in the expression *to be* or *to become inured to*, this means you have learned to put up with something, you don't let it bug you any more. You might be inured to someone's rudeness, to the long queues in the supermarket, to the awfulness of Friday-night television or to anything else unpleasant that has been around for a long time and isn't going to go away.

❦

juncture
Related to *junction* and other words to do with joining, this means a point at which events converge and thus an important point in time: 'At this *juncture*, I can't confirm or deny the report, but I hope to make an announcement by the end of the day.'

❦

kowtow
A Chinese word for a sign of deference (to a monarch or the like) that historically involved touching the forehead to the ground. Nowadays you don't have to bow so low (or indeed at all) to *kowtow* to someone, but you do have to obey them implicitly, in a servile manner. To *kowtow* to your boss is not merely to do as you are told, but to do it without question, grovellingly, even when the boss is wrong or unreasonable. See also SUBSERVIENT.

❦

lacerate
To tear the flesh off – 'The whipping left severe *lacerations* on his back and legs' – or, figuratively, to wound somebody's feelings, to be very cutting: 'The comedian's *lacerating* wit made a lot of the audience feel uncomfortable.' Not to be confused with *macerate,* which means to soak something, particularly fruit, in order to soften it: 'The cherries had been *macerating* in wine for twenty-four hours and were deliciously alcoholic.'

Macerate in its turn is not be confused with *masticate*, which is absolutely not connected to any other word that has just come into your mind. It means to chew thoroughly.

৩✺৩

largesse

Generosity – often in handing out money on a special occasion, but also in bestowing gifts or favours. The bestowing is frequently done by a monarch or a government and has traditionally been rather lavish or flamboyant; of late a note of disapproval has crept into the word, so that *largesse* is not only lavish but possibly more than the giver can afford.

৩✺৩

lucrative

Lucre, often used facetiously and prefixed by the adjective 'filthy', simply means money. *Lucrative* is the adjective derived from it and can be used with no suggestion of facetiousness or filth. *Lucrative employment* is well-paid; *a lucrative investment* will show a healthy profit.

৩✺৩

manifold

Think of the first part of this word as *many* and the second in the same sense as *threefold* or *a hundredfold* and the meaning becomes obvious: 'having many parts, many different kinds'. You might describe someone you admired as having *manifold virtues* or a flower show as having *manifold varieties of rose*. You should probably make sure you say it jokily, though, or it may sound a bit formal or stilted.

৩✺৩

ministration

This is the noun derived from *ministering*, in the sense of *ministering to someone's needs*. It's therefore kinder and more caring than most forms of *administration*, to which it is closely related in terms of its derivation.

❦

mitigate

To make milder or less severe: 'Your apology may have *mitigated* her anger, but you should try not to annoy her again.' In a court of law or elsewhere, *mitigating circumstances* may enable you to get off more lightly. Not to be confused with *militate*, often followed by *against* and meaning to have significant effect or weigh heavily: 'Your confession *militates* against the evidence that showed you were nowhere near the scene of the crime.'

❦

modicum

A bit, a small quantity, often used of an abstract quality: 'If you had a *modicum* of common sense you would have closed the windows before it started to rain' or 'With only a *modicum* of knitting skill you can make attractive and unusual presents.'

❦

mollify

To soothe, to make less harsh or angry: 'I know you're trying to *mollify* me by bringing me flowers, but I'm still upset' or 'Dad was only slightly *mollified* by my assurance that my unruly friends would be leaving first thing in the morning.'

myriad

From a Greek word meaning 10,000, this now just means lots. Lots and lots. It can be an adjective – 'You'd have *myriad* opportunities if only you would fill in the application form' – or a noun – 'a *myriad* of daffodils seemed to have appeared in the park overnight'.

☙

nemesis

According to the Greek historian Hesiod, Nemesis was a daughter of Night and the goddess of retribution: if you annoyed the gods with your insolence (a crime otherwise known as HUBRIS), it was Nemesis who meted out an appropriate punishment. In modern parlance (and often without the initial capital), *nemesis* is the person or thing who brings you your comeuppance – as Harry Potter did to Voldemort, for example. You don't even need to have done something bad: the insect pest phylloxera, notorious for its destruction of grape crops, may be seen at the *nemesis of vine-growers*, or even of vines.

☙

obviate

From Latin words meaning 'to go against, to act contrary to', this is most commonly used in the expression *to obviate the need* or *necessity* to do something: 'Her having texted me *obviates* the necessity for me to speak to her.' In other words, it renders it unnecessary – I don't need to do it.

☙

palliative

Palliative care may be given to someone nearing the end of their life: it relieves pain without curing the disease.

The word can also be used in a broader sense of making something less severe: Doctor Johnson, writing in the Preface to his Dictionary about undesirable changes in language, suggested 'that we retard what we cannot repel, that we *palliate* what we cannot cure'. And, not very comfortingly, the eighteenth-century French wit Sébastien-Roch Nicolas Chamfort observed, 'Living is an illness to which sleep provides relief every sixteen hours. It's a *palliative*. Death is the remedy.'

pandemic

Like an *epidemic*, only more so: *epidemic* is literally 'among the people', the *pan* part means 'all'. This can be either a noun (*the pandemic spread all over Africa*) or an adjective, usually *a pandemic disease.* Either way, it means the affliction is found over a very wide area. It's rare to find this word applied to anything other than a disease, although the OED has two citations from the 1990s, one claiming that *wood-oven pizzas are pandemic* and the other that a certain type of music has *pandemic dance-floor appeal.* I'm inclined to prefer UBIQUITOUS in either of those contexts.

perquisite

From the Latin meaning an acquired possession, this is the word from which we get *perk*, as in *the perks of the job*; these may include a company car, a clothing allowance or free access to the gym. *Perquisite* is not to be confused with *prerequisite*, something that is required as a prior condition, which, in the case of the same job, could be a decent salary, your own office and a reasonable chance of promotion.

piquant

From the French for 'to prick', this is used to describe food that is pleasantly tasty, a little spicy, but not PUNGENT. The noun is *piquancy* and in both cases the *qu* is pronounced *k*, not *kw*. Be careful how you use these words, though: they can be a bit show-offy, analogous to referring to 'a cheeky little wine'.

Both *piquant* and *piquancy* may also be applied to the emotions, referring to something that has bite, but may also have an element of poignancy (see POIGNANT): you can add *piquancy* to conversation by introducing interesting new ideas or to a romantic situation by realizing that you aren't as young as you used to be.

plethora

CORNUCOPIAS are always depicted as overflowing with goodies, but in a bountiful, joyous way. A *plethora* goes one step further – it is a super-abundance, just too much. You might have *a plethora of overpriced restaurants* along the seafront in a holiday resort; *a plethora of advice* about career opportunities; or *a plethora of choice* in a large supermarket. All of these will have you tearing your hair, or at least moaning, 'I don't know. It's just too much!'

privation

Related to *deprive*, this means a lack of basic necessities such as food and shelter: 'The famine left the people in a state of extreme *privation*.'

prodigal

The Biblical Prodigal Son squandered his inheritance on fast living, came to grief and returned home with his metaphorical tail between his legs to a joyous welcome and the killing of the fatted calf. The part of the story that made him *prodigal* was the first bit – the lavish and extravagant lifestyle. The word can be both a noun and an adjective, so you can be *a prodigal* or *a prodigal person* or you can indulge in *prodigal spending*. Whichever way, you'll soon find yourself in trouble. There's no guarantee of a fatted calf at the end of this story.

prodigious

This is the adjective deriving from *prodigy*, a person, often a child, of outstanding talent. A prodigy can also be a thing that causes wonder – an abnormality or a freak. *Prodigious* therefore means amazing, often in the sense of 'causing amazement by its size or abundance'. The words are only loosely related to PRODIGAL, although if you are prodigal you are capable of spending a prodigious amount of money.

profligate

Another word often associated with spending lots of money, this comes from the Latin for corrupt and can mean immoral (usually in a sexual sense) as well as shamelessly extravagant. Again it can be either a noun or an adjective, so you can be either *a profligate* or *a profligate person*; you might have *a profligate lifestyle* and *be profligate in your spending*. It all sounds very tiring, and rather wasteful, too.

prolific

Describing someone as *a prolific author* is kinder than saying that they churn their books out: yes, they produce a large number, but there is no suggestion of a loss of quality. The word derives from the Latin for offspring and was originally used to describe bearing either fruit or children: you might have *a prolific apple tree* in your garden or say (probably jokingly), 'We're a *prolific* family: I have twenty-eight first cousins.' To *proliferate* – to grow or increase rapidly – comes from the same root.

Unrelated to but capable of being confused with prolific is the less complimentary adjective *prolix*, which means excessively flowing, long-winded: *a prolix author* may well be prolific, but he or she is also boringly verbose.

◦⟡◦

promulgate

Loosely used to mean 'to spread widely', this originally meant to put (a law) into effect or to proclaim something officially. Where once you might have *promulgated the news* by getting the town crier to announce it, now you could simply put it on Facebook.

◦⟡◦

propitiate

Related to *propitious*, meaning fortunate, promising good things ('The *propitious* atmosphere of the meeting made me feel the right decisions would be made'), *propitiate* means to appease, to make someone who is (or is threatening to be) against you come over to your side. In ancient times, sacrifices were made *to propitiate the gods* (particularly the Greek god of the sea, Poseidon, who could rustle up quite a storm when annoyed), but you can also

attempt *to propitiate someone* – or *propitiate their anger* –
by cooking them a nice meal or offering to help with their
latest project.

❧

proscribe

The Ancient Roman dictator Sulla was an early advocate
of *proscription* – he put a list of his enemies' names up
in a public place to announce that they were no longer
protected by law (which meant it was fine with Sulla if
anyone chose to murder them). Nowadays such bodies
as the United Nations and the European Court of Human
Rights discourage anyone from going that far, but terrorist
organizations are *proscribed* in many countries and if you
argue too loudly with your coach you may find yourself
proscribed from the golf club. It means made illegal,
banned, forbidden, and of course is not to be confused with
prescribe, which is something doctors do with medicines
or well-meaning friends do when they suggest you are
overworking and need a holiday ('I *prescribe* a week at a
health spa – you'll feel a new person').

❧

protégé

The French for protected, in English this is a noun denoting
a person under your protection or whose career you have
fostered: 'She thought of him as a *protégé*, as she had
given him his first job and helped him towards his first
promotion.' *Protégé* is the masculine form; the feminine
has another *e,* but not another accent, on the end.

❧

pungent

Like PIQUANT, this comes from a word meaning to prick,
but with reference to food it would be a decided insult: *a
pungent dish* would be too powerful by half, in both taste
and smell. *Pungent* and the noun *pungency* can also be used
in a figurative sense: *a pungent criticism*, for example, pulls
no punches.

❦

punitive

Punishing, causing hardship: *a punitive rise in prices*
would be a significant increase, one that few people could
afford; *a punitive expedition to the North Pole* might be
made more difficult by imposing a time limit or not
taking sufficient supplies. In legal terms *punitive damages*
are intended to punish the offender and deter him or her
from reoffending, rather than simply to compensate the
victim.

❦

regale

To entertain generously, either with food and drink or with
words: you could *regale* someone with champagne and
caviar, or with stories of your travels. There's a positive
implication here, too: the person you are regaling is
interested and amused. Perhaps surprisingly given the
implication of lavishness, there is no connection with
regalia; this word for the emblems and robes of high office
is related to *regal* and therefore to *royalty*.

❦

rejoinder

A reply, a riposte, especially a sharp, witty one: 'The dazzling *rejoinder* I should have made came to me half an hour later, long after I had put the phone down.'

❧

repudiate

To reject, disown or refuse to admit to: you might, if you were in the diplomatic service, *repudiate a treaty*; as a private individual you might have to content yourself with *repudiating a debt* (not only by refusing to pay it, but by asserting that you had never borrowed the money in the first place) or *repudiating a lover* (by throwing his ring back at him and not taking his calls).

❧

salutary

Connected with the Latin for health and safety, this means beneficial, leading to an improvement: if you have *a salutary experience* you will learn a lesson and think twice about doing whatever it is again. From the same root comes *salubrious*, meaning health-giving, wholesome: 'The *salubrious* seaside air soon had her feeling better.'

❧

sanction

Not a fancy word so much as a confusing one, as it has two apparently contradictory meanings. You can *impose sanctions* on a country, meaning that you refuse to trade with them; at the same time you can *sanction* (authorize) the sale of arms to them. *Sanction* comes from a Latin word meaning a decree that can't be disobeyed, so the important element of the definition is the authority, the demanding of submission, rather than whether it is for or against.

◦◦◦

schadenfreude

Literally 'harm joy' (and pronounced *shard-n-froi-duh*), this means taking pleasure in the misfortunes of others, the feeling you get not when you win but when someone else loses. The style journalist Peter York perfectly summed up the malice inherent in the word when he described the covers of the crueller type of celebrity magazine: 'The photographs show botched plastic surgery, raging eczema, weight gain and horrible clothes for maximum schadenfreude.' Because schadenfreude comes from German, some people insist on spelling it with a capital; others put it in italics. I say it's been in English long enough – well over a century – for neither of those to be necessary.

◦◦◦

serendipity

Meaning the ability to have happy accidents or make pleasant discoveries, this was coined by the eighteenth-century Gothic novelist and politician Horace Walpole; he allegedly remembered reading a Persian fairy-tale called *The Three Princes of Serendip* in which the princes possessed this gift. *Serendipity* can describe anything from your dream house coming on the market just after you have won the lottery to bumping into someone you haven't seen for years and are pleased to see again (*a serendipitous encounter*). You might also *make a serendipitous discovery*, such as accidentally finding a rich crop of mushrooms when you were out for a walk in the woods – it wouldn't be serendipitous if you had been actively looking for them.

shibboleth

According to the Biblical Book of Judges, the Ephraimite people couldn't pronounce the *sh* sound, so after the people of Gilead had defeated them in battle they (the Gileadites) devised a test to identify the Ephraimite refugees: 'Say *shibboleth* [it meant an ear of corn].' The Ephraimites did their best but could manage only *sibboleth*, as a result of which they blew their cover and were slaughtered. In modern English a *shibboleth* is something – not necessarily a word, it could be a turn of phrase or a style of dress – that distinguishes a certain class or group: 'Some of the *shibboleths* of the class system remain; it's still not easy for anyone with the "wrong" accent to get a job here.'

sinecure

From words meaning without care, this means an easy job, one that pays you money without your having to do much to earn it. It originally applied to a position within the church, but can now refer to a secular job as well: 'Not only is that seat on the board of directors a *sinecure*, it also pays for the house in France.'

sully

To make dirty, usually in a metaphorical sense: 'The scandal *sullied* what had till then been a blameless reputation' or 'Don't *sully* my daughter's ears with that filth.'

sumptuous

If you REGALE someone with food and drink, you entertain them *sumptuously*, lavishly, richly, with no expense spared.

The word can also be applied to fabric (*a sumptuous velvet*), dress (*a sumptuous costume*) or almost anything extravagantly magnificent (*a sumptuous painting of a* CORNUCOPIA).

* * *

symbiotic

Sym- or *syn-* as a prefix means 'with' (from Greek, as opposed to *com-* or *con-*, which are the Latin counterparts) and the *bio* here is the same as in *biology* or *biography*, from the Greek for 'life'. *Symbiosis* is a biological term for two plants or creatures that live together in a mutually dependent way – *a symbiotic relationship* – without either harming the other, which would be *a parasitic relationship*. The word's use now extends beyond biology to any two things or people whose close ties are beneficial to both. A productive working relationship between actor and director, for example, could be described as *symbiotic*, as could the relationship between two nations with firm trading links and no intention of invading each other.

* * *

symposium

In Ancient Greece this was a drinking party. A drinking party where intellectual conversation was the order of the day, certainly, but a drinking party nonetheless. Nowadays it is a conference at which delegates present papers or discuss a given subject. At the time of writing, the internet is advertising a *symposium* to take place in Geneva which is 'arguably the most important event in the implant dentistry calendar', so presumably those attending are ready for a few drinks afterwards.

CHAPTER SIX

Heaven, Hell and the Bits in Between

Here we have words about gods, the heavens, the end of the world, but also about the earth, nature, religion, politics, the state and its citizens and what you call it when you put your hands on your hips. I make no apology: a chapter entitled 'Heaven, Hell and the Bits in Between' was always going to have a broad remit.

accoutrements

Strictly speaking, soldiers have uniforms, weapons and ...
other stuff; that other stuff is called their *accoutrements.*
More loosely, the word can include clothing and equipment
and be applied to contexts outside the military: 'He arrived
with two assistants, a security guard, a string of limousines
and all the other *accoutrements* of the wannabe rock star.'

aegis

Normally in the expression *under the aegis of someone*,
this means under their protection or patronage: 'He was
a talented musician but it helped his career that he made
his debut under the *aegis* of his famous father.' The word
comes from classical mythology, where it signified a shield
carried by Zeus, king of the gods, or by his daughter, the
war goddess Athena.

akimbo

An odd word with a specific meaning: strictly speaking,
only the arms can be *akimbo*; it's the position they are in
when you stand with hands on hips and elbows sticking
out, away from the body. Why we need a word for this, I
have no idea. But it's now used more loosely: of the legs,
spread widely or all over the place – 'The man on the train,
legs *akimbo*, was occupying two seats and spilling over into
the aisle' – and, of more or less anything else, askew or in
disorder – 'With her skirt twisted and her hat *akimbo* on
her head, she could not have looked less like a successful
stockbroker.'

apocalyptic

The New Testament Book of Revelation, in which St
John is granted a vision of Christ's Second Coming, the
Day of Judgement and the destruction of the world, is
sometimes known as the *Apocalypse*. The word literally
means 'disclosure' (or indeed 'revelation'), but away
from the theological context it is commonly used to
mean the 'disclosure of something disastrous' or the
disaster itself, particularly when something is utterly
destroyed. *Apocalyptic* is the adjective derived from this.
Fire is a frequent feature of *apocalyptic* imagery: in his
One Summer: America 1927, Bill Bryson describes an
anti-radical politician as making 'a series of apocalyptic
speeches' in which he 'warned that the flames of revolution
were licking across the country'.

apotheosis

Note the *theo* in the middle of this word: it is from the
Greek for god and is found in *theology* and other words
connected with religion. An *apotheosis* is a deification,
making someone into a god or as least glorifying them in
an extravagant way. The nineteenth-century art historian
Anna Jameson, waxing eloquent about a painting of the
Virgin Mary, describes it as showing 'spotless grace,
ETHEREAL delicacy, benignity, refinement, repose – the very
apotheosis of womanhood'. You can also use the word in a
slightly less high-flown fashion to describe an artistic or
literary style: 'Baroque architecture reached its *apotheosis*
in the Palace of Versailles.'

cherubic

Resembling a cherub: childish and innocent-looking. *A cherubic countenance, a cherubic expression* or *a cherubic smile* would all be sweetly appealing, but – particularly when applied to a small child – might well disguise the little monster within. In Christian theology cherubs or cherubim are the second order of angels; ranking above them are the seraphs or seraphim, from whom derives the word *seraphic* – not innocent so much as serene, rapt in contemplation of the divine.

◦◈◦

climacteric

As a noun, this means a critical point in a period of history or in someone's life, particularly the moment of their highest achievement. Referring to plots against the life of Elizabeth I the historian John Cooper refers to *the climacteric of 1584* and Michael Kennedy's biography of Benjamin Britten describes the *War Requiem* as marking *the climacteric of his career*. The word may also be used as an adjective, as in *a climacteric event* or *a climacteric year in the artist's life*. It's also, bizarrely, a EUPHEMISM for the menopause.

Climacteric is often confused with *climactic*, the adjective connected with *climax*; this in turn needs to be distinguished from *climatic*, which is to do with *climate*.

◦◈◦

crepuscular

Pertaining to dusk; dimly lit. *Crepuscular animals* are active in the half-light of dawn or dusk (as opposed to *diurnal* and *nocturnal* ones, active during the day and night respectively). In a less literal sense, a badly lit room may be clad in *crepuscular gloom* or a series of dark corridors may lead you to *the crepuscular world of the academic researcher.*

෧෴௦

deluge

A flood, but a flood on a torrential scale. It can be used literally or figuratively: 'The *deluge* swept away twelve houses' or 'The announcement brought a *deluge* of protest.'

෧෴௦

demise

A euphemistic word for death: 'The harsh climate contributed to his early *demise*.' It can also be applied to the failure or end of an institution: *the demise of the nuclear family* or *the demise of the music industry*. Often used in a slightly pompous way by social commentators, or in a jocular way by those who know they may be accused of pomposity.

෧෴௦

demographic

Originally an adjective derived from *demography*, the study of human populations, their size, structure and so forth, this is now used as a noun to mean a particular sector of a population, such as makes up the audience of a television show or the readership of a magazine: 'The episode was popular among its target *demographic*, the thirty-five-plus age group, but meant nothing to anyone younger.'

෧෴௦

denizen

An old-fashioned or poetic word for an occupant or inhabitant, as in *the denizens of the forest*, who could be owls, deer or elves, depending on the context.

détente

A French word for relaxation, used in English particularly with reference to the relationship between two nations: *a marked détente in Russian–Polish relations*.

detritus

Literally, loose stones worn away from rock, bits and pieces of exploding stars or other naturally occurring debris. But the word is often used more casually to mean any sort of rubbish or leftovers, from *the detritus of a life* (all the bits and pieces that need to be sorted out after someone has died) to *the detritus of a takeaway meal* (the uneaten food and dirty containers that should have been put in the bin last night).

dignitary

This can apply to either church or state; it is related to *dignity* and means a high official, with the assumption that such a person is worthy of respect. That said, it's often used slightly ironically, as if the speaker weren't according the dignitaries much respect at all: 'Many foreign *dignitaries* were invited to the Royal Wedding' or 'There's always going to be trouble when church *dignitaries* get together and discuss their views on women priests.'

diktat

A German word related to *dictator* and *dictation*, this means a decree, an order imposed by the victor on the defeated: 'The Taliban issued a *diktat* banning the cinema in Afghanistan.' The word can also apply to a less formal but still dogmatic statement: a 2013 *Daily Telegraph* article about a proposed ban on olive oil being put on restaurant tables in glass containers was headed 'Britain must succumb to EU's new olive oil *diktat*, say officials'. That choice of word says everything the writer wanted it to say about the daftness of the regulation.

empyrean

A rather highfalutin word, this: expect people to eye you strangely if you introduce it into casual conversation. It means heavenly, relating to the heavens, but also heavenly in the sense of sublime: Wordsworth's *Prelude* refers to 'solid mountains ... drenched in empyrean light', which gives you an idea of the context in which you might use it. Equally highfalutin but worth throwing in at a time like this is the adjective *cerulean*, meaning a deep sky-blue.

ephemeral

Transitory, lasting only a short time, as in *an ephemeral pleasure*, *ephemeral success* or *the ephemeral nature of a magazine* as opposed to a hardback book.

eschatology

With its first two syllables pronounced *ess-cat*, this is the study of the end of the world and the Last Judgement. It's not used in a broader, figurative context and is perhaps therefore a bit technical for this book, but it complements the word APOCALYPTIC earlier in this section.

❧

ethereal

When it's not referring to an anaesthetic, *ether* or *aether* means the upper regions of the heavens – if something *vanishes into the aether*, it floats away like a helium balloon or an undelivered e-mail and is never seen again. (In fact, undelivered e-mails, being essentially unpoetic, almost always vanish into the *ether*, without the more romantic initial *a*.) *Ethereal* is the adjective derived from all this; it means as light as air. A tiny, delicate woman might be described as having *an ethereal beauty* and might drape herself in *fluttering, ethereal garments*.

❧

evanescent

Literally, vanishing, fading away, but often used as a synonym for EPHEMERAL – transitory, short-lived. Fame and popularity are often described as *evanescent*: here today, gone tomorrow.

❧

halcyon

From the Latin for 'kingfisher', *halcyon* means peaceful, gentle, carefree. It's usually found as part of the expression *halcyon days*, originally a period of calm weather occurring around the winter solstice, but now generally a rather ironic reference to an earlier and happier period in life: *the halcyon days of my youth*.

❧

hegemony

From the Greek for *authority*, this refers to a group or an element of society that is in the ascendant over the rest. It is usually used in an angry or resentful way: naming no names, one Middle Eastern politician is quoted as saying of another regime that it 'aims to gain *hegemony* over the entire Middle East and hold the world's economy hostage'. This is clearly not meant as a compliment.

❦

heterodoxy

Hetero- means different, other than; a *heterosexual* is one who has sex with members of the other sex and *heterodoxy* is holding views that differ from those that are widely accepted. It's the opposite of *orthodoxy*, *ortho-* meaning straight or correct. *A heterodox figure* is therefore someone who goes against received opinion, whether it's in connection with religion, economics, global warming or anything else.

❦

hierarchy

Words beginning *hier-* are generally connected with priests: *hieratic* means to do with priests; *hierocracy* is rule by priests and presumably someone once thought that Egyptian *hieroglyphics* had been carved by priests. But *hierarchy* has moved away from this sense and now means any body of people or things ranked in a specified order: *the hierarchy of the aristocracy*, for example, ranks dukes above marquesses and marquesses above viscounts; there is *a hierarchy of plant classification*, in which an order is bigger than a genus, which is in turn bigger than a species; and even this book has *a hierarchy of headings*, with the chapter titles printed in bigger type than the headings of individual entries.

⚬≋⚬

idyllic

An *idyll* is a poem or piece of prose describing an idealized country life; from that it came to mean anything idealized or particularly charming: *a romantic idyll* on a Greek island, perhaps. *Idyllic*, the adjective derived from this, can be used to describe anything from the same Greek holiday to *idyllic weather*, the kind that is not too hot, not too anything, just perfect. But, it has to be said, it probably won't last.

⚬≋⚬

incumbent

From the Latin for to lie on or to devote one's attention to, this can be either an adjective or a noun. As a noun, it means the present holder of a position, especially one in the church: 'He hopes to become bishop when the *incumbent* retires.' As an adjective, usually in the expression *incumbent upon someone to do something*, it describes a moral obligation or duty: 'It was *incumbent* upon him to look after his sister's children after she abandoned them.'

⚬≋⚬

ineffable

A word often applied to God and meaning 'too great to be explained in words'. More broadly, it can mean 'too vast to be understood, indefinable': you can experience *ineffable joy*, *ineffable peace* or, according to the Belgian novelist Georges Simenon with reference to his character Inspector Maigret, *the ineffable pleasures of pipe smoking*.

itinerant

Travelling, especially as a casual worker: 'The grape harvest depended on a number of *itinerant* employees, eager to earn money to see them through the winter.' An *itinerary*, the list of places you are going to go and times when you have to be somewhere, comes from the same root.

❧

miasma

An unhealthy atmosphere, particularly one caused by something decomposing: 'No one who lived near the swamp could avoid the *miasma* it gave off and almost everyone caught a fever.' But the word may also be used metaphorically, so that you might find Chicago in the 1920s *infected by a miasma of corruption* or the homeless *sinking into a miasma of despair.*

❧

mortification

From the Latin for 'making dead', this has a specific meaning in the Christian Church: *the mortification of the flesh* once meant self-flagellation (whipping yourself) as a way of atoning for sins; now it is more likely to mean fasting, walking barefoot or in some other way depriving your senses of GRATIFICATION. More broadly, mortification means a feeling of humiliation and a loss of self-respect: 'I was never so *mortified*,' you might say, when an embarrassing photograph was posted on Facebook; or 'He was *mortified* to hear that the bank had refused him a loan.'

❧

mundane

Of this world and therefore everyday, dull: *the mundane tasks* of shopping and housework; *the mundane routine* of driving to work, working and driving home again.

❦

nebulous

From the Latin *nebula*, which means a mist or cloud (and is used in astronomy to describe various sorts of cloud formation). The adjective means vague, hazy, having no distinct shape: *a nebulous photograph of fairies at the bottom of the garden* or 'I have a *nebulous* idea that I should have been somewhere else an hour ago, but I can't think where.'

❦

nepotism

Latin, confusingly, used the same word, *nepos*, for both a nephew and a grandson, but that is quite convenient in modern English, as *nepotism* means giving preference to any member of the family or, by extension, to friends or associates, regardless of their fitness for the position in question. 'It is pure *nepotism* that so many Harvard graduates are on the board: the Chairman knew them when they were students together.'

❦

oligarch

In modern British English, this is almost always preceded by 'Russian', although the word is Greek in origin and refers to a member of any small group that happens to be in power. Nothing in the derivation of *oligarch* has anything to do with money; what most of us mean when we talk about the people who own football or baseball clubs is a *plutocrat*, who is by definition rich.

⟨≋⟩

paraphernalia

A fancy word for 'stuff' or a less accurate one for ACCOUTREMENTS. Historically it meant a woman's property that remained hers after marriage, rather than passing to her husband; now it just means anyone's possessions or the things needed for a particular activity: 'She needed three suitcases to accommodate all the clothes and *paraphernalia* she wanted for the weekend' or 'He took a lot of *paraphernalia* when he went fishing, because he was fussy about which rod he used in various weather conditions.'

⟨≋⟩

partisan

A member of or adherent to any party or cause, particularly a resistance group: 'The *partisan* forces held out for months against the invading army.' As an adjective, therefore, *partisan* means biased, one-sided, firmly allied with one point of view against another. *A partisan crowd* – whether at a political rally or a football match – is not going to be swayed by a rousing speech or by good play by the other team; it has already decided who it wants to win.

⟨≋⟩

peregrination

Peregrine, in addition to being the name of a falcon, is an old-fashioned adjective meaning foreign or migratory. A *peregrination*, therefore, is a long, wandering journey, one that probably has no fixed *itinerary* (see ITINERANT, page 151). You might talk of *the peregrinations of Marco Polo* or, closer to home, *the girls' peregrinations around the shopping mall*, as they kept an eye out for bargains.

∽⁊⁍〜

peripatetic

From the Greek for pacing to and fro, this means wandering, but in a more organized way than ITINERANT or PEREGRINATION. *A peripatetic research fellow*, for example, might have jobs at both Oxford and Princeton and divide his time between the two. With a capital letter, *Peripatetic* also refers to the teaching or followers of the Greek philosopher Aristotle, who chose to do his lecturing while wandering about rather than sitting in a classroom or under a *stoa* or porch as the *Stoics* did.

∽⁊⁍〜

periphery

Lots of words beginning *peri-* mean something to do with enclosing or encircling: *the perimeter of a rectangle* is the measurement around all the sides, while *a perimeter fence* encloses an entire property and a *periscope* enables you to look around when you are under water. The *periphery* of an area is its outermost boundary, as in *the periphery of the village*, on the fringes but still in the built-up area; you might also be on *the periphery of society*: on the outskirts but not quite accepted. *Peripheral vision* allows you to see to the sides rather than straight in front of you; and *computer peripherals* are things like modems and keyboards that aren't an integral part of the main piece of kit.

∽⁊⁍〜

populist

In a political context, relating to the people, rather than to traditional parties or ideologies. *A populist senator* is one who claims to have – and may indeed have, who knows? – the interests of the people at heart.

༄

posthumous

After death (or, literally, after having been buried – *humus* is the Latin for earth and is the source of the word for garden compost). A writer might achieve *posthumous acclaim* if her works had not been appreciated in her lifetime; she might even have a prize *awarded posthumously*.

༄

prelapsarian

Christians refer to the Fall of Man, the moment in the Old Testament Book of Genesis when Adam and Eve, having eaten the forbidden fruit from the tree of the knowledge of good and evil, lose their innocence and are expelled by God from the Garden of Eden. Prelapsarian literally means 'before the fall' and can be used (perhaps slightly pretentiously) to refer to a state of extreme innocence, naivety or other condition in which ignorance is bliss.

༄

prerogative

A privilege belonging to a certain group, class or person: *the Royal Prerogative* is power that is, for whatever reason, in the hands of the Crown; it may be *the Chairman's prerogative* to open a meeting with a short speech and it is often *the prerogative of the father of the bride* to give his daughter away.

profane

In its least disapproving sense, *profane* simply means secular, not sacred, nothing to do with God or the Church. But the meaning has broadened to become more PEJORATIVE than that, to imply a lack of respect for religion or things religious: 'His language was so *profane* that I expected him to be struck by a thunderbolt for talking like that in a church.' More broadly still, although a *profanity* would strictly speaking be a blasphemous expression or exclamation, it can be extended to apply to any form of swearing. See also IMPRECATION.

purview

Not a million miles from a REMIT, this means the scope or range of something like a report or an inquiry. 'The relationship between the Chairman and the Treasurer is a private matter; it does not fall within the *purview* of the committee.' *Purview* isn't connected with *view*; it comes from the same root as *purvey* and *purveyor* (as in *purveyor of luxury foodstuffs to the President*) and is to do with providing or supplying.

remit

As a noun – pronounced *ree-mit*, with the emphasis on the first syllable – this means a person or group's area of authority: 'It was the agent's job to secure the best deal for her client; spending hours discussing his writer's block was beyond her *remit*.' The verb, pronounced *rimmit,* with the stress on the second syllable, means to send, especially money, hence the *remittance advice* that tells you money has been transferred to your account.

retribution

The original meaning of this word would be clearer if you put a hyphen in it: *re-tribution* was once the repayment of a service or a good deed (a *tribute*), or the return of something that had been borrowed. All entirely good things. Then the Christian Church started talking about the *Day of Retribution* or the Day of Judgement, when divine reward or punishment would be handed out – good or bad, depending on how you had behaved during this life. The modern, secular meaning is almost always negative: *retribution* is the punishment or comeuppance you get for any form of wrongdoing.

sacrilegious

Disrespectful of something sacred: 'It is *sacrilegious* (or *an act of sacrilege* or just *a sacrilege*) to wear your shoes in the temple'. You can also commit sacrilege against something secular that is worthy of great respect: 'It was *sacrilegious* to suggest that Laurence Olivier had given a bad performance.'

stricture

Related to *strict*, which in turn is connected to a Latin word for to draw tight, this means either a restriction (same derivation) or a severe criticism. NATO might *apply strictures* to the military policy of its member states, someone with an entrepreneurial spirit might set up on his own to avoid the *strictures* of a large company, while a critic might *pass strictures* on a concert he didn't enjoy.

subfusc

At some universities this is the insiders' term for the dark-hued clothes worn under an academic gown for exams and other formal occasions. Elsewhere, it's simply a rather nice adjective meaning dark or gloomy. *A subfusc industrial town* might be part of *the subfusc background of a painting*, while someone's *subfusc clothes* might fit in well with *the subfusc décor* of a dreary boarding house.

⟨≋⟩

totalitarian

Related to *total* and *totality*, this refers to a dictatorial style of government that regulates every aspect of life: 'George Orwell's *1984* is a satire on the dangers of the *totalitarian* state that tries to control how its citizens think.' Or, as the polemicist Christopher Hitchens put it, 'The *totalitarian*, to me, is the enemy … the one that wants control over the inside of your head, not just your actions and your taxes.'

⟨≋⟩

xenophobic

Anything ending in *-phobic* is related to fear and *xenophobic* means frightened of or positively hostile towards foreigners. The TOTALITARIAN state described in the previous entry would probably have a number of *xenophobic* policies, designed to stop its citizens finding out that life was better somewhere else. But an individual may also be *xenophobic* (or exhibit *xenophobia*) and thus refuse to travel abroad or learn a foreign language.

⟨≋⟩

zealot

Zeal may mean little more than 'enthusiasm', but often suggests excessive enthusiasm – acting with *reforming zeal*, for example, implies that you are instituting a *lot* of change, taking little account of the wishes of others. With a *zealot*, there is no doubt: he or she carries enthusiasm too far – particularly enthusiasm for a religious, political or social cause. The eighteenth-century poet Alexander Pope advised against it in his *Essay on Man*:

> For modes of faith let graceless *zealots* fight;
> His can't be wrong whose life is in the right.

In other words, living a good life matters more than arguing over the form religion should take. Moderation in all things …

zeitgeist

German for 'spirit of the time' (the first syllable is pronounced *zite* and the second to rhyme with 'iced') and often employed in an arty way: 'The film really captured the sixties *zeitgeist*.' Use this word, by all means, but be prepared for accusations of pretentiousness.

zenith

The *zenith* is the point in the sky lying directly above an observer and is used metaphorically to mean the high point in a person's achievements: 'His career was at its *zenith*, but his health and family life were suffering.' The opposite (unobservable in the sky) is the *nadir*, considered the lowest point to which anyone can sink: 'He reached the *nadir* of a poor season by being sent off after ten minutes.'

CHAPTER SEVEN

Science and the Arts

These are words drawn not only from science, literature and art, but also from the Classics, from French and from the study of language generally. They contain praise and criticism, greetings and, appropriately for the last chapter, farewell. How's that for careful planning?

aesthetic

Having an appreciation of beauty and good taste, especially in the arts; or, if the word is used of a thing, appealing to a person who has that appreciation. Thus a student of poetry may have *a great aesthetic SENSIBILITY*, while the poetry may be *aesthetically pleasing*. There is a movement in art called *aesthetics*, which maintains (to put it at its simplest) that beauty is more important than anything else; a person who subscribes to this view is called an *aesthete*, though this is a word that may also be applied disparagingly to someone who *thinks* they have great appreciation of the arts.

Aesthetic comes from the Greek for feeling, which also gives us *anaesthetic*, a drug that stops us feeling anything, and *synaesthesia*, a concept in psychology where you feel that an unexpected sense is being stimulated, as when a certain sound reminds you of a smell or a colour.

❦

alchemy

An ancient pseudoscience whose adherents (*alchemists*) sought a way of turning base metal into gold and of finding the *panacea* or cure for all ills, including aging and death. Today the word is used loosely to refer to any magical transformation: *the alchemy of love*; *the alchemy of make-up and sympathetic lighting*; *the alchemy of darkness that turns an inoffensive spare bedroom into a source of untold horrors*.

Mention of panacea also leads me to remark on a common TAUTOLOGY: it is wrong to talk, as many people do, of *a universal panacea*. As in PANDEMIC, *pan-* comes from the Greek for all, so if whatever it is doesn't cure everything, everywhere, it isn't a panacea.

❦

allegory

A story, painting or similar work whose characters and
content symbolize a deeper meaning than is at first
apparent. John Bunyan's seventeenth-century allegory of
the Christian's path to Heaven, *The Pilgrim's Progress*, has
characters with the expressive names of Giant Despair and
Mr Valiant-for-Truth, while George Orwell's *Animal Farm*
is an allegory of political events in Russia, with the pigs
Napoleon and Snowball representing Stalin and Trotsky
respectively. The word comes from the Greek for 'to speak
figuratively' and the related adjective is *allegorical*.

amanuensis

Originally, a secretary (in Ancient Rome, probably a
slave) employed to copy manuscripts or take dictation;
now any secretary or literary assistant: 'I couldn't have
completed the work on time without the help of my tireless
amanuensis.' (There is something about the work of an
amanuensis that makes it almost essential for him or her to
be tireless.)

anachronism

The *chron* element again comes from the Greek for time
(see CHRONIC) and the whole word means 'someone or
something out of its time'. In Shakespeare's *Julius Caesar*,
for example, there is an *anachronistic* reference to the
striking of a clock: striking clocks had been invented by
Shakespeare's time, but they didn't exist in Ancient Rome.
Period dramas are often accused of anachronistic
lines, putting modern slang into the mouths of Anne
Boleyn or Cleopatra. An institution – a golf club that

refused to accept women, for example – or an elderly person with antiquated views might also be described as an *anachronism*, but in the latter case only if you were being deliberately unkind.

❧

analogy

A comparison made to point out a similarity between two things: 'To a non-economist, the *analogy* of the brakes failing on a car might help to explain what happens when inflation runs out of control' or 'The Wild West *analogy* is a good one – that same pioneering spirit makes people want to conquer space.'

❧

anecdote

Sir Ernest Gowers' *Plain Words* points out that strictly speaking an *anecdote* is 'a story never told before, whereas we all know that now it generally means one told too often'. This is a nice distinction that has largely been lost, because to most people an anecdote is simply a story, a personal reminiscence. But the sense of 'unpublished' survives in the scientific world: *anecdotal evidence* is evidence that hasn't been written up in a paper. Once it is published, the sticklers say, it becomes *a case history*.

❧

anthropomorphic

From the Greek for 'changing into a human', this means attributing human qualities and feelings to an animal, a deity or anything impersonal. *Animal Farm*, mentioned on page 162, could be described as *anthropomorphic* in that it ascribes human characteristics to pigs and other animals;

the same could be (and has often been) said of *Watership Down* and *Bambi*.

⟋⟍

antithesis

The direct opposite, as in 'That sort of mealy-mouthed journalism was the *antithesis* of everything I had ever fought for' or 'Illegal drug-taking is the *antithesis* of the spirit of Olympic sport.' There's no need to say anything like *complete antithesis*: this is another of those words, like *panacea*, mentioned under ALCHEMY, that either is or isn't. You can't have *a partial antithesis*, so you don't need a *complete* one.

⟋⟍

apology

On a day-to-day basis, most of us know what an *apology* is: a way of saying sorry. It can also be a poor substitute for something: 'That's an *apology* for a Christmas cake – there's hardly any fruit in it.' But there's a more literary meaning, too. An apology – or, even more impressive, an *apologia* – is a formal justification of actions or opinions. In this sense an apology can be quite brazen, a justification, a standing up for yourself or someone else, with no hint of regret or asking for forgiveness. When an eighteenth-century bishop wrote *An Apology for the Bible*, it wasn't nearly as odd as it sounds to modern ears.

⟋⟍

apostrophize

In a literary context, this means to address someone or something in an *apostrophe* – a rhetorical speech that digresses from the main stream of what you were saying.

The person or thing may be real or imagined, present or absent: George Eliot writes of a character 'bursting out into wild accusing *apostrophes* to God and destiny'. This rather poetic word is connected only loosely with the more familiar and dreaded *apostrophe* found in books about punctuation.

archetype

A typical example, a perfect specimen: 'John Wayne was the *archetype* of the classic Western hero' or 'The female *archetype* has become a pagan symbol, synonymous with Mother Earth.' The adjective is *archetypical*: 'After she went back to work, he became an *archetypical* house-husband, much more domesticated and keener on cleaning than she had ever been.'

auspicious

Priests in Ancient Rome used to examine the entrails of birds to see if a certain date would be favourable for a journey or an important celebration. This was known as *reading the auspices*, and a favourable result was *auspicious*. Two thousand years later you can still – if you have the right connections – make an official visit to a foreign country *under the auspices* (protection or guidance) of the local embassy, and *an auspicious occasion* is one when it looks as if everything is going to turn out well. You might say that a festival *got off to an auspicious start* because the weather was glorious on the first day; similarly, an actor might make *an auspicious debut* if he was a success in his first role.

bathos

Anti-climax, a descent from something emotional to something banal: 'The opera descended into *bathos* when the soprano had a coughing fit during the final aria.' Not to be confused with *pathos*, which is a feeling of sorrow or sympathy, such as might be aroused by the heroine dying during the final aria.

The adjective derived from pathos is *pathetic*, which meant 'arousing sympathy' for several hundred years before it became 'contemptible'. Experts argue about whether the adjective from bathos is *bathetic* (by analogy with *pathetic*) or *bathotic* (by analogy with *chaotic*); most prefer the former.

canard

Canard (don't pronounce the 'd') is the French for duck and also for a false note in music or a false report. This last is what it means in English – a rumour for which there is no foundation: 'The *canard* was widely repeated on social media, where its veracity was not an issue.'

caveat

This is Latin for 'let him, her or it beware' and is used in this sense in the expression *caveat emptor*, 'let the buyer beware': if you buy a house without having a proper survey done, the leaky roof becomes your problem. *Caveat* is now more commonly used as a noun; it has a strict legal sense, but in common parlance it simply means a warning: 'The employment figures may be encouraging, but the government issued a *caveat* against premature optimism.'

circumlocution

Talking around something, refusing to come to the point. The Circumlocution Office in Dickens' *Little Dorrit* is notorious for the fact that nothing ever gets done there: in one of the few examples of the department giving a brief reply, the author tells us, 'It being one of the principles of the Circumlocution Office never, on any account whatever, to give a straightforward answer, Mr Barnacle said, "Possibly."' Ambrose Bierce's ACERBIC *Devil's Dictionary* defines circumlocution as 'a literary trick whereby the writer who has nothing to say breaks it gently to the reader'.

corollary

In geometry this is a proposition that follows logically from another and can readily be deduced from it. Away from maths it means much the same – one thing that springs up as a practical consequence of another: 'The rapid growth of industrial towns was an inevitable *corollary* of the establishment of factories' or 'The *corollary* of the increase in fuel prices is that food, too, will become more expensive.'

crescendo

This is a musical term for growing louder and in a non-musical sense it means just that: *a crescendo of applause* may start gently and reach a climax when the performer reappears to take a bow. The much-used *to reach a crescendo* (meaning to reach a climax or to become very loud) is wrong: if you *reach a crescendo*, you arrive at the point where you *start* playing or applauding more loudly. Pedants cling on to this distinction, but it may be that, as with ANTICIPATE, they are fighting a lost battle.

criterion

A word of Greek origin, so the plural is *criteria*, this means
a principle on which a thing is judged or assessed: 'The
criteria for a successful Victoria sponge are lightness of
texture and a well-risen appearance' or 'To satisfy the
criteria for entry, applicants must have a good second
degree and a proven aptitude for research.'

❧

dilettante

This comes from Italian, so is pronounced as four syllables
– roughly *dill-y-tant-y*. It means someone who dabbles,
who studies or works at a subject superficially: 'Unless he
learns to get up in the morning and practise the piano for
hours a day, he'll never be more than a *dilettante*.' Although
dilettantism is usually practised in the arts, it can also have
a wider application: the American journalist Joe Klein
has written about 'this *dilettante* notion that the global
economy is evil because big corporate leaders make too
much money'. He could have said *half-baked* or *glib* and
meant much the same thing.

❧

elision

A technical word from the world of grammar, included
here because so many of us do it all the time. It means the
omission of a letter or a syllable from a word, as in *don't*
or *shouldn't*, but also in the careless pronunciation of, for
example, *secretree* for *secretary* or *proberly* for *probably*. If
this makes you feel guilty, take comfort from the thought
that you are in good company: all those *o'ers* and *'gainsts*
and *i'faiths* in Shakespeare are further examples of elision.

❧

empirical

Practical as opposed to theoretical; derived from experiment or observation: 'The *empirical* evidence is that this drug is effective, but it hasn't yet been through a clinical trial.' The word sometimes has a derogatory tone, suggesting that the observation isn't very systematic – an experienced gardener, for example, might have *empirical knowledge* but little understanding of botany. *Empirical* derives from a Greek word for a doctor who relied on observation rather than philosophy; it is not related to *empire* or *imperial*.

◦≋◦

epicurean

Epicurus was a Greek philosopher who rated pleasure highly on the list of important things in life. Students of philosophy will (rightly) say that there was more to his doctrine than that, but *epicurean* has come to mean interested in luxurious sensual pleasures, especially good food and drink. The word can be either a noun or an adjective, so you can *be an epicurean* or *have epicurean taste in wine*. Or, if you're taking your *epicureanism* seriously, both.

◦≋◦

epitome

Pronounced as four syllables, with the emphasis on the second – *ep*-it-*om*-ee – this means a person or thing that is a perfect example or embodiment of a quality or a class: 'He is the *epitome* of a laid-back man' or 'Helen of Troy was the *epitome* of the beautiful woman who can lead men astray.' In day-to-day use the distinction between this and an ARCHETYPE is a hair-splitting one: etymologically speaking, an archetype is the *original* model or example, whereas an epitome has become the *perfect* example. You wouldn't describe someone as *an* epitome of a laid-back man; the word requires the more definite, absolute qualification *the.*

⟨✎⟩

eponymous

An *eponym* (from the Greek for 'significant name') is the name of the person after whom a place, discovery, invention or the like is named: George III's consort Queen Charlotte is the *eponym* of Charlottesville, Virginia, while the French educator Louis Braille is the eponym of the writing system for the blind. *Eponymous* is the adjective derived from this, so Braille is *the eponymous inventor of braille.* The word can also be used of the title characters in books, plays, etc: Oliver Twist is the eponymous hero of a Dickens novel, though – contrary to what a lot of people believe – Pip is not. He is certainly the PROTAGONIST of *Great Expectations*, but would be the eponymous hero only if the book were called *Pip.*

⟨✎⟩

exponential

A term from mathematics that in the wider world just means 'very rapid', as in *an exponential rise in prices.* Don't say this in front of mathematicians, because they'll probably explain to you that it's to do with an *exponent,* which in turn is to do with the number of times a number is to be multiplied by itself and is *way* beyond the scope of this book.

⟨✎⟩

extrapolate

This is another mathematical term that has passed into the wider language. The Collins definition is particularly neat: 'to infer (something not known) by using but not strictly deducing from the known facts'. You may be discussing anything from the economy to the reasons for a friend's decision to pack in her job and move to Malawi; the moment someone says, 'I'm extrapolating here', you know that they are one step away from making it up as they go along. Don't quote them.

೧≋೦

gloss

Nothing to do with shiny paint, this other meaning of gloss derives from the Latin for an unusual word that needs explanation; it's related to *glossary*, a list explaining technical terms. A *gloss* in the margin of a medieval manuscript might have been the English translation of a Greek expression or some other such explanatory note. In a less formal context, it can simply mean an interpretation or comment: 'She didn't tell me all this – I'm just giving you my *gloss* on the situation.'

೧≋೦

hagiography

Strictly speaking, this means writing about saints, but has come to mean any biography that is noticeably uncritical of its subject: 'It's a complete *hagiography* – it makes no mention of her gambling or the appalling way she treated her first husband.'

೧≋೦

hedonism

In philosophy *Hedonism* is a school of thought that maintains that the pursuit of pleasure is the highest good. Quite how the philosophers justify that, I can't tell you, and the word is more widely used in a less specific sense. It means the indulging of sensual pleasures – sex, obviously, but also perhaps having a gin and tonic in a lavender-scented bath or lying in bed all Sunday morning with the papers and a few croissants.

juxtaposition

Putting one thing side by side with another, particularly if the two things are INCONGRUOUS or contrasting. 'The *juxtaposition* of their holiday homes meant that they saw more of each other than either would have wished' or 'The *juxtaposition* of the beautiful countryside with the war-torn villages was particularly troubling.' *Juxtaposition* is also a literary or artistic device, putting contrasting phrases or shades together for effect, as in the opening lines of Dickens' *A Tale of Two Cities*: 'It was the best of times, it was the worst of times, it was the age of wisdom, it was the age of foolishness' and so on.

lexicon

A dictionary or, more loosely, the particular vocabulary of an individual, a group or a branch of knowledge: 'The word "failure" isn't in my *lexicon*; let's give it another go.'

methodology

Often used casually to mean little more than *method*, this is strictly either the *study* of method or the methods applied in a certain field of activity: *the methodology of the experiments*, for example, or *the methodology of food labelling in supermarkets.*

❦

mnemonic

From the Greek for memory and with the initial *m* silent, this is what might also be described as an *aide-mémoire*; specifically a rhyme or memorable sentence that helps you to remember ... things you need to remember. Rinse Out Your Greasy Bottles In Vinegar is a *mnemonic* for the variations of the rainbow (the initials of the words give you red, orange, yellow, green, blue, indigo and violet in the right order), while Divorced, Beheaded, Died, Divorced, Beheaded, Survived is an easy enough rhyme to guide you through the fates of the six wives of Henry VIII.

❦

nuance

The French word for a shade or hue, this is used in English to mean a shade of meaning, a subtle distinction. Sir Ernest Gowers' *Plain Words*, originally intended as a guide to help members of the Civil Service write clear English, includes the view, 'The things an official has to say are in the main concerned with telling people what they may or may not do ... there is no room here for experiments with hints and *nuances*.'

❦

paradigm

A representative example or stereotype, as in 'So much of science is influenced by *paradigms* and pre-conceived ideas that it is sometimes difficult to recognize a genuine breakthrough.' In science, *a paradigm shift* is a complete change in the basic understanding of a subject, and the expression is also used in a broader context: 'Identifying science fiction and fantasy as a saleable genre was a *paradigm* shift for many publishers who had previously turned up their noses at it.'

parlance

A person or sector's way of speaking, with particular reference to choice of words or idiom: 'It reached its APOTHEOSIS or, in common *parlance*, its high point' or 'In economic *parlance*, investment tends to have a more specific meaning than it does for the rest of us.'

patois

The French for dialect, pronounced *pat-wa*. In English it means any regional variation from the written language, or the jargon of a particular group. The author Raymond Chandler famously wrote to his publisher, complaining about 'the purist who reads your proofs': 'I write in a sort of broken-down *patois* … [and] when I split an infinitive, God damn it, I split it so it will stay split.'

pedantry

The habit of insisting on formal rules, with no scope for imagination or flexibility. A person who does this is a *pedant* and what they do is *pedantic*. These tend to be subjective words – what you call pedantry I may say is merely obeying the rules. Indeed, to call someone a pedant used to be a bit of an insult, but over the last few years, with all the media debate about the importance of 'correct' English, pedants are coming into their own and flying their nit-picking flags with pride.

୧≋ତ

pithy

Brief and to the point, but whereas a LACONIC remark is laid back, a *pithy* one is sharp and forceful. The witticisms of Oscar Wilde and Groucho Marx are widely quoted, but the actor/cowboy Will Rogers was also renowned for pithy comments. They included, 'Even if you're on the right track, you'll get run over if you just sit there' and 'Politics has become so expensive that it takes a lot of money even to be defeated.' *Pithy* is related to the white *pith* of an orange; the word can also mean vigour or energy, which is what Hamlet had in mind when he talked about 'enterprises of great pith and moment'.

୧≋ତ

portentous

A *portent* is an omen, a sign of something important and possibly disastrous to come. *Portentous*, therefore, means ominous or threatening – *portentous events* may be angry meetings on street corners just before a riot breaks out and *portentous music* in a horror film may indicate that the monster is going to leap out any second now. But the word's meaning has extended to include *speaking in portentous tones*, which would be self-important and authoritative without necessarily *portending* anything dreadful.

୧≋ତ

primeval

Strictly, belonging to the first age of the world; more loosely, ancient and primitive. *A primeval desert* may have existed since the beginning of time or at least for longer than anyone can calculate; *to feel a primeval urge* to jump for joy is simply to express a very basic, unsophisticated instinct.

If anything, *primordial* is even older than primeval: it comes not from the first age but from the first beginnings. In biochemistry, there is a theory of *primordial soup*, a rich organic liquid from which, some say, life developed; less technically you may feel *primordial desires*, which would have no veneer of civilization or etiquette.

❧

protagonist

A main character in a story, whether hero or villain: Bilbo is the protagonist of *The Hobbit*, as Alex is of *A Clockwork Orange*. The Greek *protos* means first and recurs in words such as *prototype*, the first example of a product to be manufactured. This derivation means it's ridiculous to describe someone as *the main protagonist*, because there is no other kind.

❧

quixotic

Resembling the character of Don Quixote de la Mancha, created by the Spanish novelist Miguel de Cervantes. Don Quixote longs to be a knight errant and perform acts of chivalry – among his many foolish exploits he attacks a group of windmills, having convinced himself they are giants. So the adjective derived from him means idealistic but impractical and foolhardy: 'It's *quixotic* to believe in an equal society when there is such a gulf between rich and poor.'

rococo

Originally an elaborately ornamental style of architecture; later applied to various other art forms from painting to music to garden design. It may now (loosely) be used to anything that is very decorative and pretty in a rather over-the-top way.

Sisyphean

Sisyphus upset the gods (always a bad idea in Ancient Greece) and was punished by having to roll a rock up a hillside for all eternity; every time he neared the top the rock slipped and rolled back down to the bottom. A *Herculean* task, named after the Labours of Hercules, is enormous, seemingly impossible, but with enough hard work you can just about pull it off. A *Sisyphean* one is utterly hopeless.

tangent

If you draw a straight line so that it just touches but doesn't cross the circumference of a curve, that is a *tangent*. To *go off at a tangent*, therefore, is to head in a different direction, usually by introducing a new and apparently unrelated topic of conversation: 'The moment you mention Italy, even if you are talking politics or economics, he'll go off at a *tangent* and tell you how he nearly bought a vineyard in Umbria.'

tantalize

Tantalus is another figure from classical mythology (see
STENTORIAN and SISYPHEAN). Like Sisyphus, he offended the
gods; his punishment was to suffer perpetual hunger and
thirst, with water below him and a bunch of grapes above,
always receding as he reached for them and thus remaining
tantalizingly out of his reach. To *tantalize* someone, then, is
to torment them with the promise of something unattainable
or to raise their hopes only to dash them again: 'She kept him
dancing attendance on her with the *tantalizing* suggestion
that she would probably marry him one day' or 'The film's
tantalizing ending left the audience longing for a sequel.'

tautology

It always amuses commentators on language that there
should be so many words for saying the same thing twice:
a *tautology* may also be described as a *redundancy*, a
pleonasm or a *prolixity*. It simply means using unnecessary
words without adding anything to the meaning: *a brand-
new innovation*, perhaps, when an innovation is by
definition new; or *a variety of different hats*, when the
meaning of different is included in variety. The word is
often used sarcastically: *an expensive meal in a Michelin-
starred restaurant* or *an overpaid Hollywood star* may be
regarded as tautology on the basis that such meals are
always expensive and such stars invariably overpaid.

tenable

Literally, able to be held, usually used of an opinion that
can be defended against attack: 'Not everyone is going to
agree with you, but I think it is a *tenable* point of view.'

timbre

Pronounced as a French word (something like *tam-bruh*), this means a tone, a particular quality of music or voice. A nineteenth-century citation in the OED, from a doctor called William Markham, explains it beautifully:

> The voices of individuals, and the sounds of musical instruments, differ, not only in strength, clearness, and pitch, but (and particularly) in that quality also for which there is no common distinctive expression, but which is known as the tone, the character, or *timbre* of the voice.

⌒≋⌒

valedictory

Said in farewell, as in *a valedictory speech*. It can also be a noun, so a farewell speech might simply be *a valedictory*. Valedictories are spoken at the North American graduation ceremonies known as Commencement; the speaker, chosen because he or she is the outstanding student of the year, is the *valedictorian*. A happy note on which to end.

Acknowledgements

I'm grateful to Ann, John, Anne & Derek and Ros & Sam for suggesting words to be included. But my most significant debt is to my favourite comfort-read author, the incomparable Georgette Heyer, whose splendid vocabulary made compiling the contents list a much less arduous job than it might otherwise have been.

Thanks also to Louise, George, Ana and the rest of the Michael O'Mara team for continuing to think that I am a good thing and for producing such a handsome book.

Bibliography

Bierce, Ambrose *The Devil's Dictionary* (first published 1911; reissued by The Folio Society, 2003)

Bryson, Bill *One Summer: America 1927* (Doubleday, 2013)

Cooper, John *The Queen's Agent: Francis Walsingham at the court of Elizabeth I* (Faber & Faber, 2011)

Flavell, Linda and Roger *Dictionary of Word Origins* (Kyle Cathie, 1993, revised 2008)

Foyle, Christopher *Foyle's Philavery* (Chambers, 2007)

Gowers, Sir Ernest *Plain Words: a guide to the use of English* (revised and updated by Rebecca Gowers, Particular Books, 2014)

Definitions in the text are adapted from those given in *The Oxford English Dictionary* online (www.oed.com), *The Chambers Dictionary, Collins English Dictionary* and *Oxford English Reference Dictionary*. www.brainyquote. com and sentence.yourdictionary.com were also sources of inspiration.

Index

Words in **bold** are main entries.